SARA ASK & LISA BJÄRBO

VERY VEGGIE

FAMILY COOKBOOK

First published in the United Kingdom in 2015 by
Pavilion
1 Gower Street
London
WC1E 6HD

ISBN 978-1-910496-22-0

A CIP catalogue record for this book is available from the British Library.

10 9 8 7 6 5 4 3 2 1

Reproduction by Mission, Hong Kong
Printed by Toppan Leefung Printing Ltd, China

This book can be ordered direct from the publisher at www.pavilionbooks.com

Photography by Ulrika Pousette
Graphic design and illustrations by Katy Kimbell

The publisher would like to thank Frida Green for her work on this book.

First published in Sweden in 2014 by Ordfront as Mera Vego

www.ordfrontforlag.se
forlaget@ordfrontforlag.se

NOTES
Note that some recipes contain raw or lightly cooked eggs. The young, elderly,
pregnant women and anyone with an immune-deficiency disease should avoid these,
because of the slight risk of salmonella.

CONTENTS

MORE VEG for the people

Why are you reading this book? If we were to take a guess, we'd say: your daughter has announced that she's become a vegetarian? You need to learn to cook some new dishes? You feel sorry for the animals? You're just fed up with meat? You think it's ecologically sound to eat more vegetarian food? You have health reasons? Ethical reasons? Economic reasons? Perhaps you see vegetarian food as the new black? Or you just thought the cover was nice? If you already have your reasons, that's fine – but, actually, it doesn't matter if you don't.

There's a list overleaf of reasons why you might consider switching to a vegetarian diet, and more and more people agree with some or all of these suggestions, especially those with young families. But what if we focus purely on practical issues? Then we probably end up in the supermarket, on a completely normal, grey weekday afternoon, perhaps by the meat counter, next to someone who has started glancing towards the vegetable section and who's asking themselves: do we really need to eat meat today (again)? Isn't there something we could do instead?

For many, it ends with that glance, because it's difficult enough to figure out meals to cook, buy everything you need, combine the ingredients into a dish that's on the table at a decent time, that no one around the table is intolerant to and that everyone would at least consider trying. You don't need another factor. Because what on earth do you cook if you also have to make sure the food is vegetarian? Will everyone be full up? Will they get all the nutrients they need? Does everything have to be in shades of brown, and every meal consist of a wholesome pile of lentils?

Relax. We have filled this book with food that we love to cook and eat with our families: tasty vegetarian dishes that will appeal to the three-year-old, the teenager, the parent and the sceptical elderly relative, all at the same time. Some can be whipped up on a weekday in 15 minutes, with grumpy toddlers hanging around your feet. Others call for more time, but will be more luxurious and worth that extra effort.

So just try it – we hope you'll find dishes here that can become your favourites too.

Sara Ask & Lisa Bjärbo

9 REASONS to EAT MORE Vegetarian FOOD.

1 IT'S GOOD FOR THE CLIMATE AND THE ENVIRONMENT

Meat production is responsible for almost one-fifth of the world's total emission of greenhouse gases, and livestock farming is extremely demanding on our resources. Eating less meat and more vegetables is a good way to lower your negative impact on the climate and make a real difference.

2 IT'S EASIER TO VARY YOUR MEALS

If you expand your repertoire of food-that-I-cook to contain more vegetarian dishes, it's a lot easier to vary what you serve at the dinner table.

3 YOU DON'T HAVE TO SUPPORT THE ANIMAL INDUSTRY

Even if the conditions in which animals are reared are good in some countries, that's not the case in all – there are many examples of factories where animals are suffering. If you choose vegetarian food, you lower the risk that your dinner has contributed to this.

4 IT'S TASTY

There are vegetarian dishes that are so scrumptious that you almost have to cry out with happiness when you're eating them. It would be sad if you missed out on these.

5 IT'S GOOD FOR YOUR BODY

What's good for your health is, of course, relative and individual, but if you eat completely vegetarian, you lower the chances of contracting, for example, cardiovascular disease, diabetes and some types of cancer.

6 ANIMALS ARE SO CUTE

Go to Google images and search for things such as 'lamb with bottle' or 'calf on wobbly legs', and you'll see. Very cute. Very alive. Sometimes it might just feel easier to devour an onion instead.

7 YOU CAN EAT MORE CHEAPLY

Unless you insist on buying lots of meat-replacement products that cost a fortune, or on feeding yourself solely on luxurious cheeses, there's a good chance that your vegetarian meal will end up being surprisingly inexpensive.

8 YOU WON'T GET FOOD POISONING

As often, at least – especially if you go for eating vegan – because most cases of food poisoning are due to bacterial growth in animal products.

9 VEGETABLES ARE COLOURFUL

Compare the meat counter with the area for fruit and veg and you'll see. And the important thing about colours is that they aren't just beautiful, they're healthy too. The different colours contribute different protective compounds to your diet, so the more (natural) colours you manage to fit onto your plate, the better. It's easier if you eat vegetarian.

VEGETARIAN – WHAT DOES IT MEAN?

The word 'vegetarian' actually means plant-based food. In conversation, however, we usually mean 'lacto-ovo-vegetarian' – milk, eggs and vegetables – when we talk about 'vegetarian food', and this is also our starting point in this book. It means that the recipes don't contain meat, fish or fowl, but that they sometimes contain dairy products and eggs. There are also vegan recipes – which are completely free from animal products – as well as recipes that are easy to adapt to suit vegans. These we've marked as 'vegan friendly'. There are no meat-replacement products like Quorn or soya mince in any of the recipes.

WILL THE WHOLE FAMILY REALLY EAT THIS?

It would be stupid of us to promise that every member of every family will like all the recipes in this book, because that's obviously not true. People like different things, and children are the most challenging of all to satisfy at the dinner table, especially when it comes to new dishes that they don't recognize.

We tried to keep the whole family in mind when we developed these recipes. Some of the dishes are clearly aimed more towards children, some more towards adults. We think that's okay when cooking for a family. Sometimes those who like pancakes will be the happiest, sometimes those who like chilli. And regardless of this, it's always fun if everyone tries a bit.

CHILDREN AND VEGETARIAN FOOD – DOES IT WORK?

One of the most common questions that

pops up if you mention the word 'children' in the same sentence as 'vegetarian food' is whether vegetarian food actually contains enough nutrients to keep children healthy. Or, in slightly less refined words, 'Won't the child starve to death?'.

You can dismiss any worries you might have. Vegetarian food is excellent for feeding children and even babies. If you want to feed your family exclusively on vegetarian or vegan food it can be a good idea to do some research, so that you learn how to get enough variation in your diet, and which foods are particularly nutritious and therefore warrant regular inclusion. Actually, that piece of advice goes for everyone, omnivores included.

BUT WHAT ABOUT PROTEIN?

Protein is an important building block for the body, and is present in all cells. It's important to get enough protein to maintain good health and to build new cells and muscles. Sometimes people start to wave little red warning flags and shout things about protein deficiency when you mention vegetarian food. But don't worry. There is plenty of good protein in vegetarian food: in beans, lentils, peas and soya bean products such as tofu, in nuts, seeds, quinoa, cheese, egg and milk – to name but a few. The truth is you have to work quite hard to become protein deficient in the developed world. For instance, one study showed that omnivorous Nordic children get two or three times more protein than they need, so nowadays it's probably more likely that people in the developed world get too much protein than too little. And, as long as you don't plan to just eat macaroni and ketchup for the rest of your life, you can just relax. There is no chance that anyone in your family will suffer from protein deficiency from good vegetarian food.

AND IRON?

The human body likes iron. If it doesn't get enough iron it gets tired and refuses to produce red blood cells, and that's not a good situation in any way. In vegetarian food there's iron in, for example, peas, lentils, beans, tofu and other soya products, nuts, seeds (especially pumpkin seeds), quinoa, green leafy vegetables, egg yolks and dried fruit (especially dried apricots).

But if you should take those who shout 'protein deficiency' with a pinch of salt, you should actually take people who yell 'iron deficiency' a little more seriously. If you eat a strict vegetarian diet it's a good idea to remember your sources of iron, especially as those foods often contain a lot of other nutrients as well. And it's also good to eat something that's rich in vitamin C at the same time. If you do, it's easier for your body to absorb the kind of iron that's found in vegetables. Vitamin C can be found in most vegetables, fruits and berries.

WHY SO MUCH RAPESEED OIL?

We prefer to use rapeseed oil in our recipes, and we do this because rapeseed oil is a good source of omega-3. Omega-3 is an important fatty acid that the body can't produce on its own, so we have to get from the food we eat. And since vegetarian food contains a very small amount of omega-3, it can be a good idea to replace, for example, olive oil or butter with rapeseed oil.

MAT

SPARRISSOPPA
JORDÄRTSKOCKA m. RIS
UGNSPANNKAKA
DILLBÖNDIPPA m. KRYDDPRITS
PASTA med OSTSÅS

Asparagi
Verdi
€

CHAOTIC DAYS

There are weekdays when there just isn't enough time – or enough energy, for that matter. When the family is so hungry that the food should have been served 15 minutes ago, the worktop is covered with dirty dishes from the morning, and you can't find the potato peeler even though you've looked right down in the bottom of the vegetable basket, just in case. These weekdays do happen, and then you'll have to eat sandwiches and yogurt for dinner.

But then there are weekdays that are a couple of notches better. When you would consider spending half an hour, but not a second more, to get a substantial meal cooked and on the table. Here's a selection of recipes for those occasions.

SWEETCORN MINI PANCAKES

WITH COCONUT MILK

Large pancakes, mini pancakes or waffles? If the kids in our families were in charge of the dinner menu, no more variation than that would be necessary – ever. But as grown-ups, we tend to crave something new. When that happens, you can try this recipe.

1. Mix together the flour and salt in a bowl. Add the coconut milk and eggs and whisk to a smooth batter. Add the sweetcorn and sweet chilli sauce and mix well.
2. Heat a little oil in a frying pan over a medium heat and fry spoonfuls of the batter in batches to make small pancakes. Keep them warm in a low oven while you continue to fry the pancakes.
3. Stir most of the coriander into the yogurt.
4. Serve the pancakes with a few sweetcorn kernels, a dollop of sweet chilli sauce and the remaining coriander, with the rest of the sauce served separately.

SERVES 3–4
120g/4¼oz/scant 1 cup plain flour
2 pinches of salt
400ml/14fl oz/1¾ cups coconut milk
2 eggs
180g/6¼oz/heaped 1¼ cups sweetcorn
1–2 tbsp sweet chilli sauce
oil, for frying

To serve
½ bunch of coriander leaves, chopped
150g/5½oz/generous ½ cup thick yogurt (10% fat)
4 tbsp sweetcorn
sweet chilli sauce

WHAT'S THAT? I DON'T WANT IT!
When children are between two and five years old they are at their most sceptical towards new dishes and flavours. This is when the neophobia – fear of anything new – is at its worst and it can be difficult to get them to try new dishes. Patience is the key. And try introducing small helpings of new items as display food (see page 93) on the plate? It may be ignored for weeks, even months, but eventually they'll become familiar with it and give it a try.

VEGAN FRIENDLY

Choose egg-free pasta and vegan accompaniments, such as avocado, chanterelles (fried in oil), beans, sweetcorn and artichokes. Skip the tzatziki and make the almond pesto without cheese.

THOUSAND-BOWL PASTA

This is our safest bet when we need to serve food quickly to people of varying ages. Of course, mixing a pasta salad is nothing new, but here the trick is to not mix it at all. Many people (especially children) are sceptical towards everything that looks like a diffuse mess on the plate. So if you serve all the ingredients in different bowls and let everyone serve themselves to the items they want, you get around that problem. And perhaps even the most careful of dinner guests would dare to expand their repertoire of accompaniments one day?

SERVES 4

350g/12oz pasta shapes (or according to appetite)
pesto (shop-bought or homemade, see recipe right)
tzatziki (see recipe right)
5–6 different accompaniments, such as marinated artichoke hearts, halved; avocado, peeled, pitted and diced; broccoli florets, blanched for 1 minute; capers, drained and rinsed; chickpeas, cooked or tinned and drained; cucumber; kidney beans, cooked or tinned and drained; mozzarella cheese; diced chanterelle mushrooms, fried in a little oil; olives, pitted; sweetcorn kernels; small tomatoes; marinated sundried tomatoes

1. Cook the pasta according to the instructions on the packet.
2. Prepare the accompaniments.
3. Serve each ingredient in a separate bowl.

SMOOTH TZATZIKI

A tzatziki without cucumber, is that really a tzatziki? Perhaps not. But it's tasty.

SERVES 4

200g/7oz/generous 1¾ cups thick yogurt (10% fat)
2 tsp white wine vinegar
1 tbsp olive oil
½ tsp crushed garlic
1 pinch of salt

1. Mix together the yogurt, vinegar and oil.
2. Season to taste with the crushed garlic and salt.

HERBY ALMOND PESTO

It's ridiculously easy to make your own pesto: just throw all the ingredients in a bowl and blend. This is made from almonds rather than the traditional pine nuts.

SERVES 4

100g/3½oz/¾ cup whole almonds with skin on
2 handfuls of herbs, such as basil, thyme or parsley
50g/1¾oz strongly flavoured cheese, such as Parmesan
about 150ml/¼ pint/scant ⅔ cup olive oil
1 pinch of salt
a tiny squeeze of garlic purée (optional)

1. Put the almonds, herbs, cheese and oil in a deep bowl and blend until smooth with a stick blender, or pound it using a large pestle and mortar.
2. Season to taste with salt and garlic, if using.

YELLOW LENTIL SOUP
WITH COCONUT

*A soup that adapts to all different toppings. It's great
with diced peppers, toasted chickpeas or croûtons.*

1. Heat a little oil in a frying pan and fry the onion,
   carrot, curry powder and turmeric until soft.
2. Add the coconut milk, lentils and 700ml/24fl oz/
   3 cups water, bring to the boil, then simmer,
   covered, for 20 minutes until soft.
3. Leave the soup chunky or blend it until smooth,
   then return it to the pan. Add enough extra water to
   obtain the consistency you prefer.
4. Season to taste with salt, pepper and lemon or lime
   juice. Sprinkle with coriander leaves, peppers and
   chickpeas and serve with crusty bread.

 Make sure you choose a
vegan topping.

SERVES 4

rapeseed oil, for frying

1 onion, coarsely chopped

*1 large carrot, peeled and coarsely
   grated*

2–3 tsp curry powder

1 tsp turmeric

400ml/14fl oz/1¾ cups coconut milk

*200g/7oz/heaped 1 cup dried yellow
   lentils (red will work fine too)*

*salt and freshly ground black
   pepper*

juice of 1 lemon or 1 lime

To serve

*a few coriander leaves, chopped
   peppers, toasted chickpeas (see
   below) or croûtons, to garnish*

Crusty bread

TOASTED CHICKPEAS
Rinse and drain a tin of chickpeas, then toss
in a hot, dry frying pan over a medium heat for
2 minutes until lightly toasted. Drizzle with
a little olive oil, add a chopped garlic clove
and a pinch of salt and heat through to serve.

GREEN CARBONARA

A creamy pasta dish in which the traditional bacon is replaced with all sorts of green favourites, but the base of pasta, egg and Parmesan cheese remains the same. It won't be carbonara as you know it. But it will be tasty!

1. Cook the tagliatelle according to the instructions on the packet.
2. Meanwhile, boil the broccoli and asparagus in lightly salted water for a few minutes, then drain.
3. Mix the Parmesan with the egg yolks in a bowl.
4. Mix together the freshly boiled hot tagliatelle with the Parmesan mixture. Add single cream until you think the pasta is creamy enough.
5. Stir in all the vegetables and the parsley. Season to taste with salt, pepper and lemon. Garnish your plate with an extra raw egg yolk in its shell, if you like.

SERVES 4
400g/14oz tagliatelle
900g/2lb green vegetables, such as
  1 head of broccoli, chopped;
  1 bunch of asparagus, chopped;
  1 handful of mangetout;
  1 avocado, peeled, pitted
  and sliced
80g/2¼oz/1 cup freshly grated
  Parmesan cheese
3 egg yolks, plus extra for serving
  (optional)
100–200ml/3½–7fl oz/scant ½–scant
  1 cup single cream
100–200ml/3½–7fl oz/scant ½–scant
  1 cup chopped parsley leaves
salt and freshly ground black
  pepper
juice of 1 lemon

VEGETARIAN CHEESE
Standard cheeses on the cheese counter in the supermarket contain rennet, which is used to separate the curds from the whey. It is an enzyme that's extracted from the stomach of calves, so is obviously not suitable for vegetarians. However, there is an increasing number of vegetarian cheeses becoming available in many different styles. Some are clearly labelled on the front; others you may have to check the ingredients list, but you can easily substitute cheeses in all these recipes with vegetarian equivalents.

STRAWBERRY SALAD
WITH BULGUR WHEAT

Next time you're standing by the barbecue and wondering what to serve with your sizzling meats and vegetables, here's the answer. Or you can just skip the grilled meat as this filling salad will do just as well on its own, too.

1. Cook the bulgur according to the packet instructions.
2. Toast the nuts in a hot, dry frying pan, shaking the pan so they brown lightly but don't burn. Tip them out of the pan and chop them roughly, then mix them with the chickpeas and coriander in a large bowl.
3. Add the strawberries and avocados.
4. Whisk together the ingredients for the dressing.
5. Grill or fry the asparagus, corn on the cob, halloumi or portobello mushrooms, and serve with the dressing in a small bowl on the side.

Replace the honey with maple syrup and avoid halloumi.

SERVES 4

300g/10½oz/2¾ cups bulgur wheat (preferably whole, with large grains)

120g/4¼oz/1 cup hazelnuts or cashew nuts (optional)

400g/14oz tin chickpeas, rinsed and drained

1 handful of coriander or basil leaves, to taste

760g/1lb 10oz/4 cups strawberries, cut into bite-size pieces

2 avocados, peeled, pitted and cut into bite-size pieces

Honey and mustard dressing

2 tbsp olive oil

1½ tbsp clear honey (honey should not be given to children under 1 year old)

1 tbsp balsamic vinegar

1 tsp Dijon mustard

1 tsp lemon juice

salt and freshly ground black pepper

To serve

Asparagus, corn on the cob, halloumi cheese or portobello mushrooms

TERIYAKI TOFU
WITH MANGETOUT

A quick and simple Japanese-inspired tofu dish, with sweetness from the teriyaki sauce and a bit of sting from the fresh ginger. If you want to cut down on the sweetness and instead add more saltiness, reduce the amount of teriyaki sauce and increase the amount of soy sauce for the marinade.

SERVES 4

500g/1lb 2oz natural firm tofu
150ml/¼ pint/scant ⅔ cup teriyaki sauce (shop-bought or homemade – see recipe below)
2 tbsp Japanese soy sauce
2 tbsp grated fresh root ginger
rapeseed oil, for frying
115g/4oz/1¼ cups mangetout, cut into strips
a few drops of sesame oil (optional)
320g/11¼oz/2 cups egg noodles
sesame seeds, to garnish

Choose egg-free noodles.

1. Squeeze as much water out of the tofu as you can by pressing with a tea towel or kitchen paper. Press hard so that the liquid is soaked up, but not so hard that the tofu crumbles. It's easiest if the tofu has been frozen first. Dice the tofu into 1cm/¾in cubes.
2. For the marinade, mix together the teriyaki sauce, soy sauce and grated ginger in a non-metallic bowl or plastic bag. Add the tofu cubes and leave to marinate for at least 10 minutes.
3. Remove the tofu cubes from the marinade (but save the marinade).
4. Heat a little oil in a frying pan and gently fry the tofu cubes and mangetout for about 1 minute. Add a few drops of sesame oil, if using.
5. Cook the noodles according to the packet instructions.
6. Pour the remaining marinade over the noodles and stir gently, then add the tofu and mangetout and mix together carefully. Serve sprinkled with some sesame seeds.

TERIYAKI SAUCE

Ready-made teriyaki sauce is available in most supermarkets, but it's also easy to make your own. The sauce will keep fresh for several weeks in the fridge.

SERVES 4

1 large garlic clove, finely chopped
1 tbsp grated fresh root ginger
100ml/3½floz/scant ½ cup Japanese soy sauce
2 tbsp granulated sugar
2 tsp white wine vinegar or mirin (Japanese rice wine)
2 tsp potato flour

1. Mix the garlic, ginger, soy sauce, sugar, vinegar and 3 tbsp water in a pan and bring to the boil.
2. Remove from the heat and whisk in the potato flour to thicken the sauce, then pour through a sieve.

TOMATO SOUP
WITH SWEETCORN & GINGER

The nice sting in this soup comes from the fresh ginger, and if you want more of the stuff, just increase the quantity. This is really tasty! So much so that there are children (we know at least two) who list this quick soup as their absolute favourite dish.

1. Fry the onion and garlic in the oil over a low heat until soft but not browned.
2. Add the chopped tomatoes, 200ml/7fl oz/scant 1 cup of the cream, the ginger, stock cube and paprika and simmer, covered, for a few minutes.
3. Blend the soup until smooth, if you wish, and add water or cream to get a thinner consistency.
4. Add the sweetcorn to the soup and season to taste.
5. Mix the quark and wasabi together into a cream. Taste your way to the perfect sauce! The more wasabi, the sharper the flavour. Then everyone who wants to can add a spoonful of wasabi cream to their soup bowl. Sprinkle with basil.

VEGAN FRIENDLY
Replace the cream with
a soya alternative and
avoid quark.

SERVES 4

1 onion, chopped
2 garlic cloves, chopped
olive oil, for frying
2 x 400g/14oz tins chopped tomatoes
200–300ml/7–10fl oz/scant 1–1¼ cups single cream
2 tbsp grated fresh root ginger
1 vegetable stock cube
1 pinch of paprika
180g/6¼oz/heaped 1¼ cups sweetcorn, drained and rinsed
salt and freshly ground black pepper

Wasabi cream
100–200g/3½–7oz quark
a dollop of wasabi (or grated horseradish)

To serve
torn basil leaves

> **TOMATOES**
> Tinned tomatoes and tomato purée might at first sight seem like cheating. Should you not instead go out into a sun-warm greenhouse, pick a few fresh tomatoes, skin and finely chop them yourself? Purée them with your bare hands? And yes, of course that sounds lovely in many ways. But doesn't it also sound slightly, slightly unlikely that you would have the energy for that kind of ambition level on a weekday? Or even the option?
>
> In any case, there is a point to cartons and tins filled with chopped tomatoes. You see, chopped tomatoes and tomato purée are fantastic sources of the antioxidant lycopene, which has protective qualities. If you eat fresh tomatoes you won't get nearly as much of the stuff.

MINI POTATO PANCAKES
WITH THYME & FRUIT SAUCE

So, you've got loads of leftover mashed potato in the fridge? Good. If you do, this is the world's quickest, easiest and tastiest way to use it up. In Sweden, this would be served with lingonberry jam rather than cranberry sauce.

1. Mix all the ingredients together in a bowl. You should be able to form the mixture into 1cm/¾in thick mini pancakes with your hands, without it feeling too soft. If the mixture is too thin, add a little extra flour or breadcrumbs.
2. Fry the pancakes in butter or oil in either a frying pan or a pan with special small pancake moulds, until golden on both sides.
3. Serve with cranberry sauce and vegetables, such as sweetcorn, broccoli or tomatoes.

SERVES 4
mashed potato from about
  1.2kg/2lb 12oz potatoes
3 eggs
40g/1½oz/½ cup breadcrumbs
45g/1½oz/heaped ⅓ cup plain flour
1 pinch of salt
1 pinch of black pepper
1 tsp dried thyme
80g/2¾oz/1 cup Parmesan cheese or
  other strong cheese, freshly grated
butter or oil, for frying

To serve
cranberry sauce and vegetables

CHICKPEA CURRY
WITH PEANUT BUTTER & LIME

If Elvis was allowed to eat peanut butter and jam sandwiches, we're allowed to add peanut butter to our food. It's healthy too, as long as you find a peanut butter that's not made up of lots of added sugar. It's very tasty when combined in a curry with coconut and lime.

1. Cook the rice according to the packet instructions.
2. Meanwhile, fry the onion and garlic with the curry powder gently in a flameproof casserole dish.
3. Add the coconut milk, chopped tomatoes, chickpeas and peanut butter and bring to the boil, stirring. Simmer gently for a couple of minutes without a lid.
4. Stir the bananas into the curry, if using, and season to taste with soy sauce. Sprinkle with the coriander, peanuts and sambal oelek and serve with lime wedges.

SERVES 4

350g/12oz/scant 1¼ cups long-grain rice
rapeseed oil, for frying
1 red onion, finely chopped
2 garlic cloves, finely chopped
2 tsp curry powder
400ml/14fl oz/1¾ cups coconut milk
400g/14oz tin chopped tomatoes
2 x 400g/14oz tins chickpeas, rinsed and drained
55g/2oz/¼ cup peanut butter
2 bananas (optional), sliced
a dash of Japanese soy sauce

<u>To serve</u>
a handful of fresh coriander leaves
about 150g/5½oz/ heaped 1 cup chopped peanuts (optional)
sambal oelek (Malaysian chilli paste)
1 lime, cut into wedges

CHICKPEAS
You can cook your own chickpeas, if you prefer, in which case you will need about 170g/6oz/1 cup of dried chickpeas. Soak them in cold water overnight, then drain, cover with fresh water and bring to the boil. Cover and simmer for about an hour until tender. Drain and leave to cool, then you can use them or keep them in the fridge for up to 3 days, or freeze them in an airtight container.

NUT PASTA
WITH CARROT

Super quick, super easy, and heavenly for those who aren't allergic to nuts. You can, of course, flavour the crème fraîche however you wish.

1. Toast the hazelnuts in a large frying pan for about a minute until just browned. Add the oil, onion and carrots and fry gently until soft but not browned.
2. Meanwhile, cook the pasta according to the instructions on the packet. Drain.
3. Mix the tomato purée and crème fraîche, then turn the heat down and stir into the frying pan, making sure you do not allow it boil. Dilute with a dash of milk, if needed, and season to taste with salt and pepper. Add pasta and garnish with a sprig of basil.

Choose egg-free pasta and replace the crème fraîche with a soya alternative.

SERVES 4

60g/2¼oz/scant ½ cup hazelnuts (at least), coarsely chopped
rapeseed oil, for frying
1 onion, grated
3 carrots, peeled and grated
about 350g/12oz pasta, such as conchiglie
1 tbsp tomato purée
200ml/7fl oz/scant 1 cup crème fraîche
a dash of milk for thinning the sauce (you might not need this)
salt and freshly ground black pepper
a sprig of basil

NUTS
In nuts and seeds, you'll find plenty of things that the body loves: healthy fatty acids, antioxidants, proteins, fibre, vitamins and minerals – even iron! So they are really good for you – as long as you are not one of the few who are allergic. Even small children will benefit from eating nuts, but you must make sure the nuts are crushed into smaller pieces so that there is no risk of choking. And don't forget, of course, that adding different kinds of nuts and seeds is a tasty way to liven up mealtimes.

MANGO WRAPS
WITH AVOCADO

This is probably the freshest and most summery dish we know, and it's also just made for picnics. If you do make it as a picnic dish, hold off the final step, so you don't risk getting the bread soggy from the dressing. Pack the mixed mango salad in a box instead, and wrap the sandwiches once you're all set on the picnic blanket.

1. Put all the salad ingredients in a large bowl and toss together gently to mix.
2. In a separate bowl or jug, mix together the lemon juice and olive oil.
3. Add the crushed garlic and season to taste with salt and pepper.
4. Pour the dressing over the salad and stir.
5. Fill the tortillas and wrap them up!

SERVES 4

1 large or 2 small ripe mangos, peeled, pitted and diced

2 avocados, peeled, pitted and diced

1 small red onion, finely chopped

1 box of cherry tomatoes (or 3 standard tomatoes), halved or cut into wedges

a couple of handfuls of spinach, rocket or lamb's lettuce (about 30g/1oz)

400g/14oz tin chickpeas, drained and rinsed

8 tortillas

Dressing
juice of 1 lemon
3 tbsp olive oil
1 garlic clove, crushed
salt and freshly ground black pepper

PASTA ROSSO
WITH GARLIC-FRIED MUSHROOMS

The ingredients might not look the part, but do try it – it will be more delicious than you can imagine!

1. Fry the onion, 2 garlic cloves and the carrots in a large frying pan over a low heat until soft but not browned. Add the tomatoes, stock cube and crème fraîche and leave to simmer for 15–20 minutes.
2. Meanwhile cook the pasta according to the instructions on the packet. Drain.
3. Heat a knob of the butter in a frying pan and fry the mushrooms until a little dry. Add the remaining butter and garlic, then fry for another minute. Season to taste with salt and pepper.
4. Blend the sauce until smooth using a stick blender, add the oregano or basil and season to taste with salt and pepper.
5. Drain the pasta, spoon the sauce over the top and finish with the mushrooms and fresh herbs to serve.

SERVES 4

1 onion, chopped
3 garlic cloves, chopped
5 carrots (about 400g/14oz), peeled and grated
rapeseed oil, for frying
400g/14oz tin chopped tomatoes
1 vegetable stock cube
240g/8fl oz/1 cup crème fraîche
350g/12oz pasta, such as spaghetti
about 30g/1oz butter
200g/7oz button, chestnut or mixed wild mushrooms, halved
oregano or basil, to taste (fresh or dried), plus extra to serve
salt and freshly ground black pepper

 Choose egg-free pasta, replace the crème fraîche with an oat alternative and fry the mushrooms in olive oil.

TIP!
This sauce makes a perfect base for a simple veggie lasagne. Make a double batch of the sauce and layer sauce and lasagne sheets in an ovenproof dish, starting and finishing with sauce. Sprinkle with grated cheese and bake according to the instructions on the lasagne packet. Meanwhile, fry a handful of sliced mushrooms in butter and garlic and sprinkle over the finished lasagne.

GARLIC
It's a good idea to let the chopped garlic rest for a while before throwing it into the pan. That way it has time to react with the air and the protective compounds in the garlic become more active and heat resistant. In addition, chopped garlic will also be tastier than garlic that you've crushed using a garlic crusher. You can brown a finely chopped garlic clove, and the higher temperature it reaches when you do so is what it needs to taste its absolute best. Crushed garlic is too wet to be browned, so it will boil instead.

CELERY SALAD
WITH PEANUTS

Celery is one of those vegetables that people tend to either love or hate, and we'll be the first to admit that we haven't been a member of Team Celery so far. However, this salad could very well be the dish that would make us change sides. It can be enjoyed both as a main course or as a side dish.

1. Hard-boil the eggs for the dressing for 8 minutes, then plunge into cold water and leave to cool.
2. Shell and chop the eggs, then gently mix them with the rest of the dressing ingredients.
3. Prepare the salad ingredients and mix together in a bowl.
4. Serve with the dressing on the side or mix with the salad before serving, depending on what your diners prefer. Serve with with slices of crusty bread.

Choose another dressing, for example, a vinaigrette.

SERVES 4

3–4 carrots, peeled and coarsely grated
4 celery stalks, finely chopped
2–3 eating apples, cored and finely chopped
2–3 yellow or red peppers, deseeded and finely chopped
200g/7oz/1½ cups salted peanuts or walnuts (optional), chopped
150–200g/5½–7oz/1½–2 cups chopped parsley leaves
crusty bread, to serve

Mustard dressing
2 eggs
2 tbsp white wine vinegar
6 tbsp rapeseed oil
3 tsp mustard
1 tbsp granulated sugar
450g/1lb 2oz/scant 2 cups plain yogurt
2–3 garlic cloves
freshly ground black pepper

BROCCOLI PESTO
WITH PASTA & HALLOUMI

Traditionally, green pesto is made from basil, but if you're not afraid of experimenting there are endless variations to try. Here the base is made from broccoli, but the broccoli can be replaced with almost any other vegetable. Try making pesto from carrots, for example! That's also very good.

1. Toast the nuts and seeds in a dry frying pan (or skip this step and just blend them as in step 3).
2. Boil the broccoli until soft.
3. Blend the nuts, seeds and Parmesan using a stick blender, adding enough olive oil so that the pesto reaches a good consistency. Stir in the garlic and season to taste with salt and pepper.
4. Meanwhile, cook the pasta according to the instructions on the packet. Drain.
5. Cut the halloumi into cubes and fry until golden.
6. Mix together the pasta and pesto, add the halloumi cubes, grate over some Parmesan and drizzle over a few drops of lemon juice (if you're a lemon person). Garnish with a sprig of basil.

 Skip the Parmesan cheese and halloumi and serve with Toasted Chickpeas (see page 18). Choose egg-free pasta.

SERVES 4

85g/3oz/⅔ cup chopped mixed nuts, chopped almonds, pumpkin seeds or sunflower seeds – or a mixture

1 head of broccoli (about 250g/9oz), cut into florets

50g/1¾oz/½ cup Parmesan cheese, freshly grated, plus extra to serve

about 120ml/4fl oz/½ cup olive oil

1 garlic clove, finely chopped

salt and freshly ground black pepper

about 350g/12oz pasta, such as conchiglie

200g/7oz halloumi

splash of lemon juice (optional)

a few sprigs of basil

FENNEL SOUP
WITH OAT BAGELS

OK, so trying to whip up a batch of bagels on a normal weekday evening with hungry family members around your feet might not be something to recommend. But on a calm Sunday? Bagels are both tasty, beautiful and fun to bake, at least if you've got enough patience for the slightly fiddly part. And they are great for freezing, and saving for that normal weekday.

The soup on the other hand! It's so simple you can make it in a mere 15 minutes. And if you don't like the flavour of fennel you can replace it with the same quantity of broccoli.

1. Sweat the onions quickly in a little oil in a large pan until soft. Mix in the fennel and broccoli.
2. Add most of the water and the stock cube, bring to the boil, then simmer, partially covered, for 5–10 minutes until soft.
3. Add the peas and warm them through.
4. Blend the soup until smooth – it's easiest if you use a stick blender. Add a little more water until you've got the right consistency and season the soup with salt and white pepper, if needed.
5. Mix the yogurt and horseradish, mustard or wasabi and serve on the side.

SERVES 4
1 onion, roughly chopped
rapeseed oil, for frying
2 fennel bulbs, roughly chopped
1 large or 2 small broccoli heads (500g/1lb 2oz in total), cut into florets
900ml /1½ pints/3¾ cups water
1 vegetable stock cube
350g/12oz/2¾ cups frozen peas
salt and white pepper

Topping
200g/7oz/scant 1 cup thick yogurt (10% fat)
1–2 tsp grated horseradish, Dijon mustard or wasabi

Replace the yogurt with a soya
alternative.

You'll find the recipe for bagels overleaf.

OAT BAGELS
WITH AVOCADO & CREAM CHEESE

1. Crumble the yeast into a bowl. Heat the oil and water to 37°C/98.4°F and mix with the yeast. You should be able to comfortably hold your finger in the liquid without it feeling hot or cold.
2. Add the oat bran, honey, salt and flour, a little at a time, and work into a smooth and springy dough. Add more flour if needed. Cover and leave to rise for 45 minutes.
3. Turn out the dough onto a floured worktop, divide it into 12 pieces and roll each dough piece into a ball. Cover a finger in flour, stick it into each dough ball and form a bagel by spinning it around your finger.
4. Preheat the oven to 220°C/425°F/gas 7 while you leave the bagels to rise for about 15 minutes.
5. Bring about 3 litres/5¼ pints/13¼ cups water to the boil in a large saucepan and add the sugar.
6. Add a couple of bagels at a time to boil for about 2 minutes. Leave to drain, then place in a roasting pan. Continue until you have boiled all the bagels.
7. Brush with the egg white and sprinkle with the seeds. Bake in the middle of the oven for about 10 minutes until the bagels have coloured nicely.
8. Serve with cream cheese, tomato, avocado and red onion.

MAKES 12 BAGELS
25g/1oz fresh yeast
2 tbsp rapeseed oil
500ml/17fl oz/generous 2 cups water
45g/1¾oz/¾ cup oat bran
1 tbsp clear honey (honey should not be given to children under 1 year old)
1½ tsp salt
600g/1lb 5oz/4¾ cups plain flour, plus extra for dusting
2 tbsp sugar (optional)

Topping
1 egg white
100–200g/3½–7oz/¾–1⅔ cups sesame, poppy, sunflower and/or pumpkin seeds
cream cheese, tomato, avocado and red onion, to serve

 Replace the honey with syrup. Brush the bagels with soya milk, for example, instead of egg. Avoid cream cheese.

SAVE THE LEFTOVERS

The absolute quickest meals, of course, are made from leftovers that you already have in the fridge – it's something that will make both your wallet and the environment happy but it might not be especially fun or inspiring. That is, unless you take a look at these ideas and succeed in transforming dull old leftovers into something that feels brand new.

Don't chuck it... ...transform it

PASTA SAUCE » SOUP
Sweat a chopped onion, garlic and some chopped vegetables in a pan until soft, then add the leftover pasta sauce and a stock cube and leave to simmer until everything has softened. Add a dash of cream and herbs to taste and blend into a creamy soup.

SOUP » PASTA SAUCE
Heat up the soup with some chunks of marinated tofu, chickpeas or halloumi and serve as a sauce for rice or pasta.

PASTA » PASTA BAKE
Freeze leftover pasta in a large container. When you have enough, make a pasta bake with a nice cheese sauce, some Garlic-fried Mushrooms (see page 37) and Toasted Chickpeas (see page 18), for example. Or see page 52 for our Kale Pasta Bake with Blue Cheese.

RICE OR BULGUR » STIR-FRY
Stir-fry rice or bulgur with finely shredded vegetables, nuts, soy sauce and a couple of eggs. Or use the recipe on page 50.

POTATOES » WAFFLES
Cooked potato goes incredibly well in the waffle batter. Just mash them into the batter, fry potato waffles and serve with cranberry sauce or lingonberry jam. Or see page 28 for a recipe for Potato Pancakes with Thyme and Cheese.

RISOTTO » ARANCINI
Mix leftover risotto with an egg and some breadcrumbs and fry into arancini balls that are crispy on the outside and creamy in the middle. Start with 55g/2oz/heaped ⅓ cup fresh breadcrumbs, then add just enough to shape the risotto into balls.

BOILED VEGETABLES » PESTO
Using a stick blender, whizz any leftover boiled vegetables with nuts or seeds, a little garlic, olive oil and Parmesan into a pesto to serve with pasta or other dishes.

EVERYTHING ELSE » OMELETTE
Well perhaps not 'everything' else, but you can fry most things with onion and garlic, then cover in omelette batter. Or cook the mixture into a frittata in the oven.

NORMAL WEEKDAYS

So, there you are. It's a Tuesday in October and you're standing at the worktop and feeling… organised? You have about half an hour before dinner should be served, perhaps even 45 minutes. And the situation at home is under control, the washing up is sorted, the potato peeler has reappeared, you've rolled up your sleeves, and it's almost as if you've got an urge to hold your fist up high and shout something along the lines of: 'RIGHT GUYS, LET'S DO THIS, LET'S GO!'

No?

Okay, you're right, there's no need to exaggerate. Suitably ambitious weekday food – how does that sound?

BLACK-BEAN BURGERS

Chewiness, chewiness, this constant hunt for chewiness in the veggie world! It can be exhausting at times. But no one will be happy after eating a burger that just leaves a sensation of fried mash in the mouth – we can agree on that, right? Here the solution is cashew nuts that have been chopped up just enough to give a good texture.

1. If you want to serve the burger with potato wedges, make sure to get them in the oven first. (See recipe on page 97.)
2. To make the burger, fry the onion and garlic in the oil in a frying pan until soft, then add the cumin and chilli flakes and fry for a minute or so.
3. Use a stick blender to blend with half of the black beans. Season with salt and pepper.
4. Mash the potatoes into the bean mixture, then add the nuts, sweetcorn, the remaining black beans, the egg and fresh breadcrumbs. Leave the mixture to swell while you prepare the accompaniments.
5. Blend the avocado with the soured cream and season to taste with salt and garlic.
6. Shape the burger mixture into patties and toss in the panko. Fry in plenty of oil in a frying pan for 4 minutes on each side, turning with care so they don't break up. Serve with the accompaniments.

Skip the egg and the soured cream. Choose dairy-free breadcrumbs and dairy-free bread.

SERVES 4
Burgers
1 small onion, chopped
1 garlic clove
rapeseed oil, for frying
1 tsp ground cumin
¼ tbsp chilli flakes
400g/14oz tin black beans, drained and rinsed
1 pinch of black pepper
2 pinches of salt
200g/7oz mashed potatoes
75g/3oz/½ cup cashew nuts (optional), chopped
50g/1¾oz/½ cup sweetcorn
1 egg
20g/3oz/¼ cup fresh breadcrumbs
about 40g/1½oz/½ cup panko breadcrumbs (or standard breadcrumbs)

Dressing
2 avocados, peeled, pitted and cut into chunks
100ml/3½fl oz/scant ½ cup soured cream
herb seasoning salt (or regular salt)
1 garlic clove, crushed

To serve
4 burger buns
1–2 tomatoes, sliced
1 red onion, sliced
green leaves, such as spinach
Roasted Potato Wedges (see page 97), optional

PANKO

Panko is a small revolution for all cooks who like crumb-coated things extra crispy and nice. The breadcrumbs look a bit like desiccated coconut. Nowadays you can find it in most good supermarkets, either in the world foods aisle, or next to the standard breadcrumbs. You use panko just like standard breadcrumbs, but the only difference is that everything will get a little crispier, and therefore taste that little bit better.

FRIED RICE
WITH CRISPY CURRY TOFU

This is a perfect dish to make when there's leftover rice in the fridge. Of course, you can make it from freshly cooked rice too, but the result is actually even better if it's made from day-old rice that's had time to dry out.

1. Heat the oil and stir-fry the cabbage, onion, garlic, mangetout and carrots for a few minutes on high until crisp.
2. Gradually stir in the rice and continue to stir-fry until everything is mixed and the rice is hot.
3. Mix the soy sauce and sugar and stir it into the pan.
4. Mix the eggs, curry powder and salt on a plate. Put the flour and panko on two other plates. Slice the tofu into 1cm/¾in slices and turn over first in flour, then in egg and finally in panko. Heat a generous amount of oil in a frying pan and fry the tofu until crisp and golden.
5. Top the rice with the tofu slices, sprinkle with peanuts and spring onions and serve with the lime wedges, some more chopped peanuts and soy sauce.

 Leave out the eggs. Cut the tofu into cubes and turn them over in a mixture of 55g/2oz/ ½ cup cornflour, 1 tsp curry powder and 1 pinch of salt.

SERVES 4

rapeseed oil, for frying

200g/7oz white cabbage or sweetheart cabbage, shredded

1 onion, chopped

2 garlic cloves, chopped

55g/2oz/½ cup mangetout, sliced

2 carrots, peeled and finely chopped

about 600g/1lb 5oz/5 cups cooked long-grain rice, such as basmati

3 tbsp Japanese soy sauce, plus extra to serve

2 tsp sugar (optional)

2 eggs, lightly beaten

2 tsp curry powder

1 pinch of salt

55g/2oz/½ cup plain flour

55g/2oz/1 cup panko breadcrumbs (or standard breadcrumbs)

300g/12oz/10½oz firm tofu, sliced

a handful of peanuts, chopped

5–6 spring onions, sliced

1 lime, cut into wedges

TOFU
Tofu is a cheese-resembling ingredient that is made from soya beans. It's completely vegan and contains plenty of protein and loads of vitamins and minerals. It's perfect for frying, deep-frying or adding to stews. Tofu comes in different textures and flavours, from silken to firm, from natural to marinated. We often use firm, natural tofu for the recipes in this book. It doesn't taste of much on its own, so you have to do some work with spices and marinades. But it's worth it! You'll often find tofu next to the cheese counter in the food store.

KALE PASTA BAKE
WITH BLUE CHEESE

Kale and blue cheese, two tasty things that are even tastier together – if that's at all possible. If you've got leftover pasta in the fridge it's perfect to use for this bake. If not, just cook some fresh.

1. Preheat the oven to 250°C/500°F/gas 9.
2. Heat the oil and fry the kale with 1 garlic clove until soft. Spoon into an ovenproof dish.
3. Add the mushrooms and courgette to the pan and fry until the mushrooms have released their liquid, then most of the liquid has evaporated. Add the onion and remaining garlic cloves and fry until soft.
4. Meanwhile, cook the pasta according to the instructions on the packet.
5. Mix the pasta with the mushroom mixture and spread out on top of the kale in the ovenproof dish.
6. Heat the butter in a pan and stir in the flour. Whisk in the milk and cream and bring to the boil, stirring continuously. Leave to simmer gently for a couple of minutes, still stirring, until the sauce has thickened. Remove from the heat, crumble in the blue cheese and stir until melted. Season with salt and pepper, then pour over the pasta. Top with the grated cheese and bake in the middle of the oven for about 10 minutes, or until the bake has turned a nice colour. Sprinkle with thyme to serve.

SERVES 4–6

rapeseed oil, for frying
200g/7oz fresh kale, tough stalks removed
3 garlic cloves, finely chopped
100g/3½oz/1⅓ cups chanterelles or fresh mushrooms, halved
1 small courgette, cut into discs
1 onion, finely chopped
300g/10½oz pasta shapes
2 tbsp butter
3 tbsp plain flour
400ml/14fl oz/1¾ cups milk
120ml/4fl oz/½ cup single cream
140g/5oz blue cheese
salt and freshly ground black pepper
55g/2oz/scant 1 cup grated cheese, such as Edam
chopped thyme, to taste

CABBAGE
Cabbage of different kinds – and kale is of the same family – contains enzymes that are released when you cut it or chew on it. The enzyme activates compounds that protect us from disease.

DAIRY-FREE, EGG-FREE PANCAKES
FOR ENERGY, WITH ALMONDS & OATS

The secret behind successful vegan pancakes is to leave the batter to swell for about half an hour, to use enough fat and to fry at quite a high temperature so that the pancakes get a golden crust – and do use a good pancake slice.

ENERGY PANCAKES
With soya flour and rapeseed oil in the batter, these pancakes are more nutritious and give you more energy than ordinary pancakes – besides tasting delicious and being easy to flip over.

SERVES 3–4 (ABOUT 10 PANCAKES)
150g/5½oz/scant 1¼ cups plain flour, or
*   115g/4oz/scant 1 cup plain flour and*
*   55g/2oz/scant ½ cup rye flour, sifted*
4 tbsp soya flour
1½ pinches of salt
600ml/1 pint/2½ cups soya or oat milk
1 tbsp rapeseed oil
1 tsp baking powder
oil or liquid dairy-free margarine, for frying

<u>*To serve with any of the pancakes*</u>
berries, fruit salad, chocolate sauce, jam, soya
*   cream, banana slices and peanut butter or*
*   apple slices and cinnamon*

ALMOND PANCAKES
Slightly sweet pancakes with a subtle flavour of almond.

SERVES 3–4 (ABOUT 10 PANCAKES)
180g/6½oz/scant 1½ cups plain flour
55g/2oz/scant ½ cup almond flour
1½ pinches of salt
600ml/1 pint/generous 2½ cups unsweetened
*   almond milk*
1 tsp baking powder
oil or liquid dairy-free margarine, for frying

OAT PANCAKES
Oats – always yummy. And healthy too, with good fats, proteins and minerals.

SERVES 3–4 (ABOUT 10 PANCAKES)
120g/4¼oz/scant 1 cup plain flour
55g/2oz/½ cup porridge oats
1½ pinches of salt
600ml/1 pint/2½ cups oat milk
1 tsp baking powder
oil or liquid dairy-free margarine, for frying

1. Mix together all the dry ingredients except the baking powder. Add the liquid and oil, if using, and whisk to a smooth batter. Leave for 20–30 minutes.
2. Whisk in the baking powder.
3. Heat a little oil in a frying pan and add just enough batter to make a thin pancake. Fry until browned on one side, then flip it and cook the other side. It should frizzle at the edges. Add a bit more fat to the pan for each pancake and don't be stingy on the fat!
4. Serve with your choice of filling or topping as listed under the ingredients for Energy Pancakes (left).

TIP!
You can also make the soup from yellow,
green or black lentils - or a mix. Just
make sure to boil the soup until all
the lentils have softened. Green and
black lentils will need a longer cooking
time. Season after the lentils are soft
otherwise the salt can make them toughen.

ORIENTAL LENTIL SOUP
WITH OAT ROLLS

So simple to make but such a delicious concoction, this is a rich and satisfying lentil soup.

1. Sweat the onion and garlic with the curry powder and a little oil in a large saucepan until soft.
2. Add the lentils, about 1.5 litres/2½ pints/6 cups water, the stock cube and tomato purée, bring to the boil, then leave to simmer, partially covered, for 15–20 minutes until the lentils have softened.
3. Add the mixed vegetables and heat gently until all the ingredients are warmed through. Season to taste with salt, pepper and extra curry powder if necessary and serve with crusty bread.

SERVES 4
1 onion, chopped
2–3 garlic cloves, chopped
2 tsp curry powder
rapeseed oil, for frying
270g/9½oz/heaped 1 cup dried red lentils, rinsed
1 vegetable stock cube
4 tbsp tomato purée
250g/9oz frozen mixed vegetables (peas, sweetcorn and red pepper)
salt and freshly ground black pepper

To serve
crusty bread

OAT ROLLS
To make these tasty rolls, you just turn the dough out onto a floured worktop and cut the rolls out using a dough scraper or a cheese slicer. Easy peasy!

1. Crumble the yeast into a bowl. Heat the oil and 500ml/17fl oz/generous 2 cups water or milk to 37°C/98.4°F and mix with the yeast. You should be able to comfortably hold your finger in the liquid without it feeling hot or cold.
2. Add the oats, salt, sugar and flour and work into a smooth and springy, but preferably quite loose, dough. Cover and leave to rise for about 40 minutes.
3. Preheat the oven to 220°C/425°F/gas 7.
4. Turn the dough out onto a floured worktop, pat into a roll, then slice into portion-sized rolls. Leave to rise on a baking tray while the oven is heating up.
5. Bake in the middle of the oven for 10–15 minutes, or until the rolls have turned a nice golden colour.

MAKES ABOUT 18 ROLLS
25g/1oz fresh yeast
3 tbsp rapeseed oil
160g/5½oz/heaped 1½ cups porridge oats
1½ tsp salt
1 tsp sugar or clear honey (honey should not be given to children under 1 year old)
450g/1lb/scant 3¾ cups plain flour, plus extra for rolling out

 Avoid honey in the bread.

MELON SALAD
WITH FETA & OVEN-ROASTED NEW POTATOES

Frankly speaking, I wonder if it is really necessary to eat anything else but oven-roasted new potatoes. They are almost ridiculously tasty. This filling salad is best in the summer, when all the vegetables are in season and the watermelon won't cost you a fortune.

1. Preheat the oven to 220°C/425°F/gas 7.
2. Put the potatoes in an oven dish, drizzle with oil, then roast for 20–30 minutes until cooked and crisp.
3. Meanwhile, rinse the mangetout and spinach and place in a bowl with the black beans. Divide the melon in half and cut into cubes or scoop out balls using a melon baller. Stir into the salad.
4. When the potatoes are done, stir them into the salad, then crumble the feta cheese over the top. Season to taste with salt and pepper, then sprinkle with basil leaves.

SERVES 4

1kg/2lb 4oz new potatoes, halved
2–3 tbsp olive or rapeseed oil
about 100g/3½oz/1 cup mangetout
about 55g/2oz spinach
400g/14oz tin black beans, drained and rinsed
½ watermelon
150g/5oz feta cheese
salt and freshly ground black pepper
a handful of basil leaves

 Skip the feta cheese.

CREAMY THREE-BEAN MASALA

A mild but flavour-rich Indian stew: incredibly tasty for something that is so easy to prepare.

1. Cook the rice or bulgur wheat according to the instructions on the packet.
2. Sweat the carrots, onion, garlic and ginger in the oil with the garam masala for about 1 minute.
3. Add the chopped tomatoes and stock cube and leave to simmer for 10–15 minutes.
4. Add the crème fraîche and blend the sauce until smooth – this is easiest if you use a stick blender.
5. Add the beans and coriander to taste and then throw in the mozzarella. Serve with the rice or bulgur and sprinkle with cashew nuts.

Replace the crème fraîche with coconut milk and leave out the mozzarella.

SERVES 4

350g/12oz/heaped 2 cups long-grain rice or bulgur wheat

4 carrots, peeled and coarsely grated

1 onion, finely chopped

2 garlic cloves, finely chopped

1 tbsp chopped fresh ginger root (optional)

rapeseed oil, for frying

2–3 tsp garam masala

400g/14oz tin chopped tomatoes

1 vegetable stock cube

200ml/7fl oz/scant 1 cup crème fraîche

2 x 400g/14oz tins mixed beans

a handful of coriander leaves, to taste

125g/4½oz ball mozzarella cheese, diced

about 55g/2oz/½ cup chopped cashew nuts

OVEN POTATO PANCAKE

It's surprisingly easy to hide raw grated potato in a pancake batter, without the pancake-lovers around the table suspecting a single thing being different. It works for normal, thin pancakes, it works for oven pancake, and it's a very good trick to make the pancake a bit more filling and nutritious. Those who want to experiment even further can swap half of the potatoes for carrots.

1. Preheat the oven to 220°C/425°F/gas 7 and generously grease a deep roasting pan (about 35 x 40cm/14 x 16in).
2. Whisk together a pancake batter from the flour, salt, milk and egg. Stir in the potato.
3. Pour into the greased roasting pan and bake in the middle of the oven for about 25 minutes until the pancake has set and turned a nice golden colour.
4. Garnish with the basil leaves and serve with cranberry sauce.

SERVES 4–6

180g/6¼oz/scant 1½ cups plain flour
¾ tsp salt
700ml/24fl oz/3 cups milk
5 eggs
6 raw potatoes, peeled and coarsely grated
butter or oil, for greasing

To serve
a few basil leaves
cranberry sauce or lingonberry jam, and your favourite vegetables

TIP!
Does it sound a bit lonesome to eat 'only' pancake? It's nice served with red onion, tomatoes, capers, rocket and olives in small bowls on the side, for those who want extra flavour.

FALAFEL
WITH COUSCOUS PILAF

Proper falafel should really be made from chickpeas, but here we've used yellow peas instead, and we actually think it's even tastier. The thing with falafel is that the peas preferably shouldn't be cooked before preparing the falafel, just soaked. That's when you get a good texture and avoid a falafel that just tastes like fried hummus. It doesn't, of course, mean that you can't take the shortcut and buy pre-cooked peas, but the result will be better if you make it from scratch. And soaking is so easy – you just have to remember to do it in advance.

1. Soak the peas in a large bowl of water overnight in the fridge (or for at least 12 hours). They will swell when absorbing the liquid, so be generous when you choose the size of your bowl!
2. Fry the onion and garlic together with the cumin, coriander, paprika and chilli for about 1 minute, making sure the spices don't burn.
3. Drain the water off the peas and blend them with the onions, salt, parsley and lemon juice into a smooth paste, using a blender or food processor. A stick blender will work if you're stubborn.
4. Shape into meatball-sized falafels, adding a little plain flour or water to get the texture just right.
5. Sweat the vegetables for the couscous pilaf quickly in a frying pan with a few drops of olive oil. Add the couscous and stir. Pour over the water, add the salt and bring to the boil, covered.
6. Remove from the heat, leave to rest for 2 minutes, then toss, adding some more oil if needed.
7. Fry the falafel balls in oil until golden. Serve with the couscous and a sauce, such as tzatziki.

SERVES 4

Falafel balls
500g/1lb 2oz/2¾ cups yellow dried peas
1 onion, coarsely chopped
2 garlic cloves, coarsely chopped
2 tsp cumin
2 tsp ground coriander
1 tsp ground paprika
scant ⅛ tsp chilli flakes
rapeseed oil
1 tsp salt
2 handfuls of parsley leaves
juice of ½ lemon
a little plain flour, if needed

Couscous pilaf
450g/1lb vegetables, such as mangetout, peppers and onion, finely shredded (alternatively use a frozen mixture)
2 tbsp olive oil
400g/14oz/2¼ cups couscous
400ml/14fl oz/1¾ cups water
2 pinches of salt

To serve
Smooth Tzatziki (see page 17)

Make sure you use a vegan sauce.

Crispy Coated Aubergine, Courgette
and Pumpkin. See recipe overleaf.

CRISPY COATED AUBERGINE, COURGETTE & PUMPKIN

The basic idea with breading and coating things is the same no matter what kind of coating you prefer. Firstly, dip in flour, then in egg and finally in whatever you've chosen for your outer coat, for example, desiccated coconut or chopped nuts. And if you've never tried coating in Parmesan and sunflower seeds before, it's time to try now. It takes aubergine to a completely different level.

1. Rinse and cut the aubergines, courgettes and pumpkin lengthways or diagonally into half 5mm/¼in slices. If you're using pumpkin or butternut squash, make sure to peel off the thick skin. Place them on a chopping board and sprinkle with salt and pepper.
2. Place the flour, eggs and your chosen coating onto three separate plates.
3. Dip each slice into the plain flour, then in the egg and finally in the outer coating. You might have to press down the Parmesan and sunflower seed coating to make it stick.
4. Fry the vegetables in a generous amount of oil until golden on both sides in a medium-hot frying pan, then serve with rice or potato wedges and hummus or beetroot tzatziki.

SERVES 4

1–2 aubergines, 1–2 courgettes or 1 chunk of pumpkin (about 350g/12oz), or a mixture
herb seasoning salt (or regular salt) and freshly ground black pepper
90g/3oz/generous ⅔ cup plain flour
2 eggs, lightly beaten
rapeseed oil, for frying

One of the following coating options
80g/2¾oz/1 cup dried breadcrumbs with 1½ tbsp mustard powder or dried oregano
80g/2¾oz/1 cup desiccated coconut with 1–2 tsp finely grated lime zest
80g/2¾oz/1 cup Parmesan cheese and 200g/7oz/1⅓ cups sunflower seeds

To serve
Rice or potato wedges and Hummus (page 99) or Beetroot Tzatziki (page 86)

TORTIZZA
WITH THREE DIFFERENT TOPPINGS

An incredibly quick way to make your own pizza is to cheat your way around making homemade pizza dough and use ready-made tortilla breads instead. Then you can focus on the toppings and let each family-member assemble their own veggie pizza, without having to compromise on flavours.

CURRY, BANANA & PEANUT PIZZA
MAKES 4 PIZZAS

4 tortilla breads
200ml/7fl oz/scant 1 cup Tomato Sauce (ready-made or homemade, see page 71)
175g/6oz mild cheese, grated
2 tsp curry powder
2 bananas, sliced
100g/3½oz/1 cup peanuts, chopped

1. Preheat the oven to 250°C/500°F/gas 9.
2. Place the tortilla breads in a roasting pan covered with baking parchment and spread each base with tomato sauce.
3. Sprinkle with the cheese and curry powder and top with the banana and peanuts.
4. Bake in the middle of the oven for about 5 minutes, or until the cheese has melted and the pizzas have turned a nice colour.

CHANTERELLE PIZZA WITH ASPARAGUS & COURGETTE
For a fuller flavour you can sauté the chanterelles, courgette and asparagus in butter and some garlic before adding them to the pizza.

MAKES 4 PIZZAS

4 tortilla breads
200ml/7fl oz/scant 1 cup Tomato Sauce (ready-made or homemade, see page 71)
65g/2¼oz/1 cup chanterelle mushrooms
a bunch of asparagus
a chunk of courgette
175g/6oz mild cheese
a sprinkling of thyme or oregano leaves

1. Preheat the oven to 250°C/500°F/gas 9.
2. Place the tortilla breads on a baking sheet covered with baking parchment and spread each base with some of the tomato sauce.
3. Clean the chanterelles and cut them in half. Rinse the asparagus, cut off the woody ends and cut it into pieces. Rinse the courgette and slice it thinly. Add to the pizzas.
4. Sprinkle with the cheese.
5. Bake in the middle of the oven for about 5 minutes or until the cheese has melted and the pizzas have turned a nice colour. Garnish with thyme or oregano.

PESTO PIZZA WITH ARTICHOKES, TOMATO & OLIVES

MAKES 4 PIZZAS

4 tortilla breads

200ml/7fl oz/scant 1 cup Tomato Sauce (ready-made or homemade, see below)

1–2 balls mozzarella cheese, crumbled (about 175g/6oz)

115g/4oz small tomatoes, sliced

200g/7oz/3 cups mushrooms, sliced

400g/14oz tin artichokes, drained and sliced

1 handful of pitted olives

4 tbsp pesto

a couple of handfuls of rocket

1. Preheat the oven to 250°C/500°F/gas 9.
2. Put the tortillas on a baking sheet lined with baking parchment and spread each base with tomato sauce.
3. Tear the mozzarella into smaller pieces and spread out over the pizza. Arrange the tomatoes, mushrooms, artichokes and olives over the top.
4. Bake in the middle of the oven for about 5 minutes or until the cheese has melted and the pizzas have turned a nice colour. Drizzle with pesto and serve garnished with rocket.

SUPER EASY TOMATO SAUCE FOR PIZZA
Chop 1 onion and 1 garlic clove and sweat in a little oil until soft. Add 1 tbsp tomato puree and 500g/1lb 2oz tomato passata. Flavour with a vegetable stock cube, 1 tsp granulated sugar, 1 tbsp balsamic vinegar and some dried herbs, such as oregano. Leave the sauce to simmer for as long as possible – the longer it cooks the nicer it will be.

CREAMY CAULIFLOWER SOUP

WITH APPLE PANCAKES

This is a subtly flavoured cauliflower soup with potato and Jerusalem artichoke. The artichokes aren't essential, but they will contribute a delicious, luxurious flavour and a creamier consistency.

1. Clean and shred the leek and cut the cauliflower into pieces. Peel and cut the Jerusalem artichokes and potatoes into small cubes or slices.
2. Sweat the vegetables and garlic quickly in a little oil in a large pan until soft.
3. Add about water and stock cube. Bring to the boil, then simmer for 20 minutes or until everything has softened.
4. Add the cream and blend until smooth using a stick blender. Add more water until you get the required consistency and season to taste with salt and pepper. Serve garnished with pea shoots.

SERVES 4

1 small leek (about 200g/7oz)

1 large or 2 small cauliflower heads (about 700g/1lb 9oz)

3 Jerusalem artichokes

3 potatoes (preferably a floury variety)

3 garlic cloves, chopped

rapeseed oil, for frying

1.5 litres/2½ pints/6 cups water

1 vegetable stock cube

4 tbsp cream

salt and freshly ground black pepper

pea shoots, for garnishing (optional)

  Leave out the cream.

APPLE PANCAKES WITH CINNAMON

If you can, use local apples in season as these will give the best result. And if you haven't got any sifted rye flour at home, just standard plain flour will work.

1. Put the flour and salt in a bowl, add half of the milk and whisk into a smooth batter.
2. Add the rest of the milk and the eggs and whisk until smooth.
3. Peel and grate the apples and stir into the batter.
4. Fry the pancakes in a non-stick pan. Don't be stingy on the fat – they should crisp up at the edges.
5. Serve with whipped cream, cinnamon and sugar and perhaps some apple wedges to crunch on.

SERVES 4

75g/2½oz/heaped ¼ cup sifted rye flour

115g/4oz/heaped ¾ cup plain flour

2 pinches of salt

600ml/1 pint/2½ cups milk

3 eggs (or 4 if they're small)

1–2 eating apples

cooking oil, for frying

To serve

lightly whipped cream, cinnamon, sugar and apple wedges

TOFU FINGERS
WITH MASHED POTATO & CUCUMBER SAUCE

Apart from containing no fish, of course, these are so similar to fish fingers that they go under the name 'cheat fingers' in our kitchens. And what a children's favourite they are! You can flavour them as you wish by changing the marinade spices. In this recipe it's all about tarragon and lemon, but mustard or teriyaki sauce also work well.

1. Cut the tofu into sticks the same size as standard fish fingers. Squeeze out the liquid from the tofu by pressing each piece with a tea towel or kitchen paper. (More information below.)
2. Mix the soy sauce, lemon juice and tarragon for the marinade in a non-metallic bowl or plastic bag. Place the tofu sticks in the marinade and leave to marinate for 10 minutes or as long as you wish.
3. Peel and cut the potatoes into pieces, then boil them until soft in lightly salted water.
4. Beat the eggs together on a deep plate. Place the panko and flour on two separate plates.
5. Dip each tofu finger firstly into flour, then in the egg and finally in the panko. Fry them in oil for a couple of minutes on each side in a medium-hot pan.
6. When the potatoes have softened, drain off most of the water and crush the pieces into a mash with butter or margarine. Season to taste with pepper and some more salt if needed.
7. Mix together the ingredients for the sauce and serve with the tofu, vegetables, mash and lemon wedges.

SERVES 4
Tofu fingers
300g/10½oz firm, natural tofu (that's preferably been frozen)
3 tbsp Japanese soy sauce
a squeeze of lemon juice (2–3 tsp)
½ tsp dried tarragon, crushed
1–2 eggs
40g/1½oz/¾ cup panko breadcrumbs (or standard breadcrumbs)
55g/2oz/scant ½ cup plain flour
rapeseed oil, for frying

Mashed potato
1.25kg/12lb 12oz potatoes
2 tbsp butter or margarine
salt and freshly ground black pepper

Cucumber sauce
100g/3½oz cornichons
200ml/7fl oz/scant ½ cup crème fraîche
salt and lemon pepper or freshly ground black pepper

To serve
vegetables, such as carrots and radishes
a few lemon slices and dill sprigs

THE ART OF MARINATING TOFU

Tofu doesn't taste of much in itself, but it can soak up flavour from a nice marinade. For best results you will need to squeeze out as much liquid as you can from the tofu before marinating it. And it's ideal if you freeze the tofu first, and then defrost it before cooking. This makes it extra-easy to squeeze the liquid out of it.

The best way to squeeze the tofu is to use a tea towel or kitchen paper (or your hands!), and carefully press down on the tofu so that any excess liquid seeps out, but don't press it so hard that the tofu crumbles.

LASAGNE
WITH AUBERGINE & COURGETTES

Aubergine is a vegetable that doesn't taste of much itself but it's a clear winner when it comes to absorbing lots of flavour from other things. For this reason it's perfect for using in lasagne! But make sure you chop it finely, for some reason this simple weekday lasagne becomes much more delicious if you've made some effort when it comes to the chopping.

1. Preheat the oven to 220°C/425C/gas 7.
2. Sweat the aubergines, courgettes, onion and garlic in a large stir-fry pan or similar for a couple of minutes.
3. Add the crème fraîche, chopped tomatoes and vegetable stock cubes and leave to simmer for about 10 minutes. Season to taste with oregano, salt and pepper, if needed.
4. Cover the base of a 25 x 30cm/10 x 12in oven dish in sauce, so that it's just covered. Add a layer of lasagne sheets and then layer the sauce and lasagne sheets. Crumble the feta cheese in between one layer (or in half of the lasagne if the kids prefer a section without feta.) Finish with a layer of sauce. It's important there's enough sauce left over to cover the final layer of lasagne sheets, or else they'll go dry and a bit too crunchy. Sprinkle with grated cheese.
5. Bake in the middle of the oven for 20 minutes, or according to the instructions on the lasagne sheet packet. Garnish with a handful of pea shoots and olives, to serve, if you like.

SERVES 4–6

2 aubergines and 2 courgettes or other vegetables, diced
1 onion, chopped
2 garlic cloves, chopped
rapeseed oil, for frying
400ml/14oz/1⅔ cups crème fraîche
400g/14oz tin chopped tomatoes
1½ vegetable stock cubes
oregano (fresh or dried), to taste
about 12 lasagne sheets (dried)
150g/5½oz feta cheese (optional)
about 90g/3oz/1 cup grated cheese
a few pea shoots and olives, to garnish (optional)
salt and freshly ground black pepper

RED LENTIL AND COCONUT CURRY
WITH NAAN BREAD

Make naan when you have time and pop it in the freezer. It's worth making a large batch of curry as well – it's great for the lunch box.

1. Cook the rice according to the packet instructions.
2. Sweat the onion, garlic and curry paste in a little oil in a large pan for about a minute.
3. Add 400–500ml/14–17fl oz/1⅔–generous 2 cups water, the lentils, coconut milk and tomato purée. Leave to simmer, partially covered, for 10 minutes.
4. Add the cauliflower florets, return to a simmer and continue to cook for a further 10 minutes.
5. Season, stir in the spinach and heat through. Serve with nuts, lime wedges, naan bread and rice.

SERVES 4
400g/14oz/2¼ cups rice
1 onion, chopped
2 garlic cloves, chopped
1–2 tsp red curry paste
rapeseed oil, for frying
200g/7oz/heaped 1 cup dried red lentils
400ml/14fl oz/1¾ cups coconut milk
2 tbsp tomato purée
½ cauliflower head (about 250g/9oz), cut into florets
salt and freshly ground black pepper
a couple of handfuls of spinach (fresh or frozen)
120g/4½oz/1 cup cashew nuts (optional)
1 lime, cut into wedges

NAAN BREAD

1. Crumble the yeast into a bowl. Heat the oil and milk or water to 37°C/98.4°F and mix with the yeast. You should be able to comfortably hold your finger in the liquid without it feeling hot or cold.
2. Add the egg, salt, sugar or honey and flour and work into a smooth and springy dough. Cover and leave to rise for about 40 minutes.
3. Turn the dough onto a floured worktop and divide into 12. Stretch and roll out into long, flat naan breads. Put on a baking tray and leave to rise while the oven is heating up to 250°C/500°F/gas 9.
3. Bake in the middle of the oven for about 5 minutes until they've 'popped up' a little and turned a nice colour. Leave to cool on a rack.

MAKES ABOUT 12
25g/1oz fresh yeast
4 tbsp rapeseed oil
400ml/14fl oz/1¾ cups milk or water
1 egg
¾ tsp salt
1 tsp sugar or honey (honey should not be given to children under 1 year old)
600g/1lb 4oz/4¾ cups plain flour, plus extra for rolling out

Leave out the egg and choose water instead of milk and sugar instead of honey.

VEGGIE NUGGETS

WITH CURRY MANGO DIP

If a new food looks exactly the same as something children normally love, there's an increased chance that they will try it. It's very possible that this is applicable to adults too. If you prefer, you can shape the mixture into patties instead.

1. Cook the quinoa in 200ml/7fl oz/scant 1 cup unsalted water in a large saucepan, covered, for 15–20 minutes until tender. Drain.
2. Mix the onion with eggs, almond flour, cheese, soy sauce and pepper. Stir in the cooked quinoa and the breadcrumbs.
3. Cut the carrots into chip-shaped strips. Cook the potato fries according to the instructions on the packet and leave the carrots to roast with the fries.
4. Form the nugget paste into nugget shapes and fry for a couple of minutes on each side in a medium-hot pan. Don't be stingy on the oil, the surface should get crispy and golden. For optimal texture, leave the nuggets to cool slightly before serving.
5. Mix together the ingredients for the dipping sauce and serve with the nuggets and fries.

Replace the egg, cheese, breadcrumbs and almond flour with 300g/10½oz/scant 1¾ cups blended chickpeas. Form into nuggets and fry, then serve with guacamole or other dips.

HOMEMADE FRIES
It's very nice to make you own fries from crispy kohlrabi! Peel and cut into strips, place in a deep roasting pan, drizzle with olive oil and salt and bake in the oven at 220°C/425F/gas 7 until golden - about 20 minutes.

SERVES 4

Nuggets
90g/3oz/heaped ½ cup quinoa
½ onion, chopped
2 eggs
120g/4¼oz/scant 1 cup almond flour
60g/2¼oz strong hard cheese
2 tsp Japanese soy sauce
1 pinch of white or black pepper
3 tbsp breadcrumbs
rapeseed oil, for frying

Fries
4 portions potato fries
2–3 carrots

Dipping sauce
200g/7oz/scant 1 cup thick yogurt (10% fat)
3 tbsp mango chutney (or mango purée from a baby food jar for a milder dip)
½ tsp curry powder

BOLOGNESE
MADE FROM BLACK LENTILS

When we ran out of red lentils during our first recipe test, a bag of black beluga lentils in the cupboard was brought into action as a substitute. And it was the best emergency solution we've ever tried, because this really has turned into one of our new favourite dishes. Try it!

1. Sweat the carrot, onion and garlic in a little oil in a frying pan until soft. Add the lentils, tomatoes, crème fraîche, stock cube, sugar, balsamic vinegar and cumin, if using. Stir in 200ml/7fl oz/scant 1 cup water and bring to the boil.
2. Leave to simmer, partially covered, for 25 minutes, or until you think the lentils have a good texture.
3. Blend the sauce using a stick blender, or leave to simmer for a little longer before blending for a smoother consistency. Dilute with water if you want a thinner sauce. Boil the pasta while the sauce is finishing off cooking.
4. Season the sauce with salt and pepper and serve on top of the pasta with Parmesan and basil.

SERVES 4–6
1 carrot, peeled and coarsely grated
1 onion, chopped
1–2 garlic cloves, chopped
rapeseed oil, for frying
175g/6oz/1 cup black beluga lentils (can be found in most standard food shops)
400g/14oz tin chopped tomatoes
200ml/7fl oz/scant 1 cup crème fraîche
1 vegetable stock cube
1 tsp sugar
1 tbsp balsamic vinegar (optional)
some cumin powder, if you're a fan
about 350g/12oz spaghetti
salt and freshly ground black pepper

To serve
Parmesan cheese (optional)
a little basil or oregano

Choose egg-free pasta and swap the crème fraîche for an oat alternative.

PULSES
Pulses is the collective name for peas, lentils and beans, and other vegetables that grow in pods. The boring thing with pulses is that they neither sound or look particularly appetizing. Who wants to eat a colourless mulch of lentils? But if you look at what is contained in these little rascals, it's a different story. You see, pulses are packed with vitamins, minerals, anti-oxidants and super fibre. Besides, they're very filling. Oh, and there's also that thing about them often being very tasty too - something that shouldn't be forgotten.

MINI SUNFLOWER PANCAKES
WITH GREEN PEA PURÉE

Seeds are jam-packed with nutritional stuff like good fats, protein, B-vitamins, iron and zinc. This is a clever (and very tasty!) way to sneak them into your diet. Here the pancakes are served as a main, with pea purée and vegetables. But they actually work just as well together with jam and whipped cream, since they're so neutral in flavour.

1. Put the seeds and half the milk in a bowl and blend until smooth, using a stick blender if you wish. Add the flour, salt, eggs and the rest of the milk and whisk into a batter.
2. Fry as mini pancakes in a medium-hot pan, making sure not to be stingy with the fat. It's good if the edges crisp up!
3. Blend the peas and avocados to a smooth purée. Season to taste with salt, garlic and lemon juice, if using.
4. Serve the pancakes immediately with the pea purée, sunflower greens, tomatoes, pomegranate seeds and pea shoots.

SERVES 4

Mini sunflower pancakes
175g/6oz/1¼ cups natural sunflower seeds
600ml/1 pint/2½ cups milk
120g/4¼oz/scant 1 cup plain flour
1 pinch of salt
3 eggs
oil, for frying

Pea purée
200g/7oz/1½ cups frozen peas
2 avocados, peeled, pitted and chopped
1 pinch of salt or herb seasoning salt
crushed garlic, to taste
a squeeze of lemon juice (optional)

To serve
sunflower greens, tomatoes, pomegranate seeds and pea shoots

PUMPKIN VEGGIE PATTIES
WITH OVEN-ROASTED NEW POTATOES & BEETROOT TZATZIKI

Take it slowly when you blend the pumpkin seeds into the patty mixture so that the texture doesn't go completely smooth. Leaving the seeds chunky means they will give that subtle, longed-for chewiness that vegetarian patties so often lack.

1. Preheat the oven to 220°C/425°F/gas 7.
2. Put the potatoes in a deep roasting pan and drizzle with the oil. Season with salt and pepper and stir to coat the potatoes in the seasoned oil. Roast in the middle of the oven for about 25 minutes, or until they've got a nice colour and texture.
3. Mix the beetroot with the yogurt and vinegar and add a little garlic and salt to taste.
4. Sweat the onion and garlic in a little oil in a pan until soft. Put in a bowl with the beans, salt, pepper and herbs and blend until smooth.
5. Add the pumpkin seeds and continue to blend, but not too much – it's nice to have some chewiness. Stir in the breadcrumbs.
6. Form into patties and fry in a frying pan over medium heat. Serve with the potatoes, salad and tzatziki.

Replace the yogurt with a soya alternative.

Oven-roasted potatoes
1kg/2lb 4oz new potatoes, halved or quartered
4 tbsp olive oil
salt and freshly ground black pepper

Beetroot tzatziki
1 raw beetroot, peeled and coarsely grated
200g/7oz/scant 1 cup thick yogurt (10% fat)
2 tsp white wine vinegar
a little crushed garlic
salt

Pumpkin veggie patties
1 onion, chopped
1 garlic clove, chopped
rapeseed or olive oil, for frying
400g/14oz tin butter beans
2 pinches of salt
1 pinch of white pepper
2 tsp oregano or thyme leaves
210g/7½oz/1½ cups pumpkin seeds
2 tbsp fresh breadcrumbs

To serve
a fresh green salad

GNOCCHI
WITH ROASTED BUTTERNUT SQUASH

Butternut squash is tastier than pumpkin, more festive than courgette, and perfect if you're the type of person who likes to Instagram pictures of good-looking vegetables. This is a mild and slightly buttery dish that goes well with either potato gnocchi or tagliatelle.

1. Preheat the oven to 250°C/500°F/gas 9.
2. Put the squash in a deep roasting pan, drizzle with oil, sprinkle with salt and stir. Roast for 30 minutes in the top of the oven, stirring occasionally so that it doesn't stick, until slightly mushy and coloured.
3. When the pumpkin starts to look ready, sprinkle with pumpkin seeds and roast for a few more minutes, to make the seeds nice and crunchy.
4. Sweat the garlic in a little oil quickly in a pan, add the crème fraîche, water and stock cube and bring to the boil. Add the roasted butternut squash and stir.
5. Cook the gnocchi according to the instructions on the packet.
6. Season the sauce to taste with oregano, salt and pepper. Serve on top of the gnocchi with the sliced tomatoes and oregano to garnish.

Replace crème fraîche with a soya alternative and serve with potatoes or egg-free pasta.

SERVES 4
1 butternut squash, about 1.2kg/2lb 10oz, peeled, seeded and diced
4 tbsp olive oil
1 tsp salt
60g/2¼oz/½ cup pumpkin seeds
1–2 garlic cloves, chopped
oil, for frying
200ml/7fl oz/scant 1 cup crème fraîche
100ml/3½fl oz/scant ½ cup water
½ vegetable stock cube
about 650g/1lb 7oz fresh gnocchi
a sprinkling of oregano (fresh or dried)
salt and freshly ground black pepper
cherry tomatoes, sliced

BUTTERNUT SQUASH
This is a winter squash that resembles a standard pumpkin both in look and flavour. It's mild, slightly sweet and nutty, and super delicious to roast in the oven. And beautiful! As long as there is no damage to the skin it will keep fresh for weeks, so you can leave it out as an ornament in the fruit bowl for half the winter if you want. You'll find butternut squash in the vegetable aisle of good supermarkets during the winter months.

ALMOND BALLS
WITH POTATO & JERUSALEM ARTICHOKE MASH

Every time we make these meatball-resembling creations we think how practical it is that there are so many, because then we can put some in the freezer to save. Then we put them out onto the table, hear a faint rustle, and 20 minutes later each and every almond ball is gone. A shame for the idea of freezing them, but cheering all the same!

1. Peel and cut the potatoes and Jerusalem artichokes into pieces. Boil in lightly salted water for 10–15 minutes until softened.
2. Meanwhile, thoroughly blend the almonds, beans, eggs, garlic, onion, salt, pepper, pesto and cheese. Stir in the breadcrumbs and leave to swell for 2 minutes – the mixture should be firm enough to be rolled into balls. Add more breadcrumbs if needed.
3. Roll into about 45 small balls and cook a batch at a time in boiling water for 2 minutes until they rise to the surface. If you are short of time, skip this step. The balls might then be a bit gooier in the middle and slightly less round.
4. Fry the balls in a little oil in a medium-hot pan until they've got a slightly golden crust.
5. Drain off most of the water from the potatoes and Jerusalem artichokes and crush into a mash. Add butter to taste and salt and pepper, if needed. Serve with the almond balls, cranberry sauce and fresh vegetables.

SERVES 4

Potato & Jerusalem artichoke mash
12 floury potatoes (about 1.1kg/2lb 7oz unpeeled weight)
3–4 Jerusalem artichokes (can be replaced with potatoes)
2–3 tbsp butter or margarine for the mash

Almond balls
200g/7oz/heaped 1½ cups almonds
100g/3½oz/⅔ cup tinned butter beans
2 eggs
2 garlic cloves
1 small onion
½ tsp salt
1 pinch of black pepper
1–2 tbsp red or green pesto
40g/1½oz/½ cup cheese, grated
3 tbsp breadcrumbs (or more)
oil, for frying

To serve
cranberry sauce or lingonberry jam, and tasty vegetables such as broccoli, sweetcorn and mangetout.

JERUSALEM ARTICHOKE
This vegetable is actually a kind of sunflower, with small rugged tubers growing under the ground. It's the tubers you eat, almost like potatoes. Jerusalem artichoke is a bit fiddly to peel, but apart from that there isn't much not to like about it. It's actually ridiculously tasty and very nutritious. Apart from plenty of iron, it also contains a special fibre - inulin - which makes it a favourite food for the good bacteria in the gut. Try oven roasting Jerusalem artichoke, or slice it thinly and serve it in a salad.

TIP!
You can also serve the almond
balls in pitta bread, with
hummus and vegetables.

CHILDREN, flavour & new FOOD

How nice it would be if there was a definitive list of 50 recipes that all kids in the whole world love; ten tips for dinner-table peace that work for all families; and five super tricks that transform every food-refuser into a food-lover overnight.

And peace on earth! That would be nice too. But no, life is more complicated than that!

Some children eat very well, they sit properly at the table and are happy to try most things that are served. Others don't. Unfortunately we can't promise that all the recipes in this book will appeal to all children, because they won't. But we can share a few thoughts and tips that help us cope during those periods – months, years! – when the kids seem to think it's enough to eat nothing but macaroni.

1 BE PATIENT

Most children are sceptical towards new food. It's probably a throwback from the time when the whole of nature was our larder and you couldn't just scoff down the first mushroom you found, because it could turn out to be poisonous. The most difficult are the years between two and five years old. Then it often passes over, slowly but surely. Be patient! And keep serving the food that you want the kids to grow to like – if you don't, they'll never learn.

2 KEEP FOODS SEPARATE

Stews and foods that are mixed together are rarely popular, probably because it's difficult to see what's gone into the mixture. Often it's easier to learn to like food that's divided up into several small bowls. The taco model in other words. You can apply this to loads of different meals.

3 TRY THE SMOOTH APPROACH

A tomato soup with chunks of onion might feel a bit easier to try if it's blended so it is creamy and smooth – and garnished with something familiar. Many pasta sauces can also be blended. Children seem to like the idea that food is cooked from one sole ingredient.

4 INTRODUCE DISPLAY FOOD

Learning to like a new flavour requires that you dare try it – one, two, three, yes perhaps over 20 times. Some children find this difficult, but they may respond to a dollop of it added onto the edge of the plate. We call it display food – food to get used to. One day the display food will get eaten.

5 TRUST YOUR CHILD

Studies show that children are happy to eat unvaried food each mealtime. But seen over a longer period of time (weeks and months) there's often a good balance. Trust the child! You're responsible for good and healthy food being served at the table and the child is responsible for what and how much he or she wants to eat.

6 LET CHILDREN HELP

Many children would rather eat food that they've helped to prepare. Make some time at the weekend to involve them in the process.

7 WERE YOU A PICKY EATER?

Were you also picky with food as a child? Fussiness is hereditary and nothing to be ashamed of. You turned into a decent human being after all, right? Take a few deep breaths instead of nagging until you turn blue. It's often then, when you look away, that the breakthroughs happen.

8 CONSIDER TASTE SENSITIVITY

Some children, and adults, are extra sensitive to certain tastes, especially to bitterness. Olives, grapefruit, Brussels sprouts and broccoli taste even more bitter for them. And since bitterness is associated with poison, it easily grinds to a halt there. These children need even more preparation and more sample tastings before a new flavour appeals. And you'll need even more patience.

9 TRY NOT TO NAG

Nagging the kids about eating up their food is often counter-productive – there's even scientific proof of that. Besides, it's incredibly boring. A little reminder that there's food on the plate, and that it's time to eat it now is fine, but try to keep the nagging to a minimum.

10 LISTEN TO HUNGER SIGNALS

Children are often better than us adults at listening to their hunger and fullness signals. Do treasure these! Let the child have control over how much they have on their plate.

11 BE A GOOD ROLE MODEL

Adults are children's best role models. Sit properly at the table, eat vegetables, try the new food and show that you think it feels safe and tastes nice – then you increase the chances that the children will follow suit. Not today, not tomorrow, but eventually…

WEEKEND AT LAST

Suddenly it happens! The weekend arrives, you've got time, you're feeling in the groove. This is when you cook the dishes in this chapter. Those that might need a touch of extra love, but which will return the favour in the form of feel-good weekend vibes when you're done.

TAPAS

Tapas is the Spanish name for small dishes – it actually means a 'lid' because they used to serve slices of ham or other foods on top of a glass of sherry in the bars. It is a concept that provides an infinite number of possibilities so everyone in the family should like at least one dish that's on the table. Here are six of our favourites.

COURGETTE ROLLS WITH HALLOUMI
SERVES 4

1 small onion, finely chopped
1 garlic clove, finely chopped
olive oil, for frying
400g/14oz tinned chopped tomatoes
4 tbsp white wine
1 medium-sized courgette, trimmed
200g/7oz halloumi cheese
1 pinch of sugar
salt and freshly ground black pepper
1 handful of chopped basil or thyme leaves

1. Preheat the oven to 220°C/425°F/gas 7.
2. Sweat the onion and garlic in a little oil in a pan. Add the chopped tomatoes and wine and leave to simmer gently.
3. Using a cheese slicer, cut the courgette into long, thin slices.
4. Cut the halloumi to give you the same number of cheese sticks as courgette slices. Roll one cheese stick into each courgette slice. Line up the rolls in a 15 x 25cm/6 x 10in ovenproof dish.
5. Season the tomato sauce to taste with some sugar, salt, pepper and herbs. Pour the sauce over the courgette rolls and bake them in the middle of the oven for about 20 minutes.

ROASTED POTATO WEDGES
SERVES 4

1kg/2lb 4oz potatoes suitable for roasting
3½ tbsp olive oil
salt and freshly ground black pepper

1. Preheat the oven to 220°C/425°F/gas 7.
2. Rinse the potatoes and cut into wedges. Place them in a deep roasting pan, drizzle with olive oil and season with salt and pepper. Toss so the potatoes are coated in seasoned oil.
3. Roast in the middle of the oven for about 30 minutes until the potatoes have coloured. Flip them over twice during roasting, so they don't stick.

CHILLI AIOLI (FOR THE ROASTED POTATOES)
MAKES 250ML/9FL OZ/GENEROUS 1 CUP

2 egg yolks
1 tbsp white wine vinegar
1 tsp Dijon mustard
240ml/8fl oz/1 cup rapeseed oil
a little crushed garlic
1 pinch of chilli flakes

1. Mix together the egg yolks, vinegar and mustard in a sturdy bowl – it should be so heavy that you don't have to hold it while whisking.
2. Pour the oil into a jug or similar and very slowly drizzle it into the egg mixture, whisking vigorously until it thickens.
3. Season to taste with garlic and chilli flakes and dip the potato wedges into it.

More recipes overleaf »

ARTICHOKES WITH LEMON BUTTER
SERVES 4

4 artichokes (large or small)
1½ tsp salt per 1 litre/1¾ pints/2½ cups water
80g/2¾oz butter, at room temperature
juice of 1 lemon
freshly ground black or pink pepper (optional)

1. Rinse the artichokes thoroughly.
   Remove the stalk and the bottom leaves.
   Boil in lightly salted water for about
   40 minutes for large or 25 minutes
   for small artichokes. Take out with a
   slotted spoon and let the water drain off.
2. Flavour the butter with lemon and
   perhaps some pepper and serve with the
   artichokes.

GARLIC-FRIED MUSHROOMS
SERVES 4

300g/10½oz/5 cups mushrooms, quartered
  or diced
2 tbsp olive oil
2–3 garlic cloves, chopped
2 tbsp balsamic vinegar
3 tbsp chopped parsley leaves
salt and freshly ground black pepper

1. Heat up a frying pan and add the
   mushrooms. Leave to fry for a few
   minutes until most of the liquid has
   evaporated. Then add the oil and garlic
   and continue frying for another minute
   or two.
2. Add the balsamic vinegar and parsley
   and season to taste with salt and pepper.

PUFF PASTRY SPINACH & FETA DUMPLINGS
MAKES 20 SMALL DUMPLINGS

2 shallots, finely chopped
100g/3½oz spinach
a little olive oil
150g/5½oz feta cheese, crumbled
paprika
about 250g/9oz puff-pastry sheets
a little flour, for dusting
salt and freshly ground black pepper

1. Preheat the oven to 200°C/400°C/gas 6.
2. Sweat the shallots and spinach in a
   drizzle of oil in a stir-fry pan.
3. Add the feta cheese and season to taste
   with salt, pepper and paprika.
4. Spread the pastry on a lightly floured
   surface and cut out 9cm/3½in rounds
   using a cookie cutter or a glass. Add a
   spoonful of filling to each one, dampen
   the edges and pinch the edges of the
   pastry together. It's important you don't
   fill them all the way to the edges, or the
   dumplings will break apart when you
   bake them.
5. Bake in the middle of the oven for about
   10 minutes until they have turned a
   nice, slightly golden colour. They taste
   best when served warm but not too hot.

ROASTED VEGETABLES
IN PITTA BREAD

We love vegetables that have been roasted on a tray until perfectly crispy – so tasty! They make a complete meal with hummus, but if you want more food in your pitta bread you can add Falafel (page 64) or Almond Balls (page 90).

SERVES 4

at least 500g/1lb 2oz diced vegetables, such as broccoli, cauliflower, courgette, asparagus, aubergine, onion and pepper (enough to fill a deep roasting pan)

2 garlic cloves, chopped

3½ tbsp olive oil

salt

75g/3oz/½ cup pumpkin or sunflower seeds (optional)

4–6 pitta breads (shop-bought or homemade, see recipe overleaf)

1. Preheat the oven to 250°C/500°F/gas 9.
2. Cut the vegetables into quite small, similar-sized cubes, discarding any woody stems.
3. Place the vegetables and garlic in a deep roasting pan. You should have enough vegetables to fill the tray but not much more – they will need some space to roast properly. Drizzle over plenty of olive oil, sprinkle with some salt and toss together.
4. Roast in the top of the oven for 15–20 minutes until the vegetables have coloured nicely, stirring occasionally. Towards the end of the roasting, sprinkle the seeds over the vegetables to let them get a bit of colour, too.

5. Fill the pitta breads with vegetables and hummus to serve.

HUMMUS WITH TOASTED SESAME SEEDS
Oh, this yummy dip, packed with nutrients! If there's any leftover from dinner you'll be happy, because you can use it for spreading onto your sandwiches or as a dip for veggie sticks. And if you want to make a milder hummus, just leave out the cumin from the recipe.

SERVES 4

5 tbsp sesame seeds

2 x 400g/14oz tins chickpeas, drained and rinsed

1–2 garlic cloves, chopped

100ml/3½fl oz/scant ½ cup olive oil

juice of 1 lemon or lime (optional)

salt, paprika and ground cumin, to taste

1. Toast the sesame seeds in a dry frying pan until golden, then tip into a bowl. Be careful they don't burn.
2. Using a stick blender or ordinary blender, blitz the seeds, chickpeas, garlic and oil until smooth.
3. Add lemon or lime juice, salt, ground paprika and cumin to taste.

More recipes overleaf »

PITTA BREADS

1. Crumble the yeast into a bowl. Heat the oil and water to 37°C/98°F and mix with the yeast. You should be able to comfortably hold your finger in the liquid without it feeling hot or cold.
2. Add the flour, a little at a time, with the salt and sugar and work the mixture into a smooth and springy dough.
3. Cover the dough with oiled clingfilm and leave to rise in a warm place for about 45 minutes.
4. Preheat the oven to maximum.
5. Turn the dough out onto a floured worktop. Divide the dough into 20 pieces and roll or press each one out into a circle. Place in a roasting pan and leave to rise for another 20 minutes.
6. Bake in the middle of the oven at until the breads have puffed up and turned a nice colour, about 6 minutes. Keep an eye out as this can happen very quickly!
7. Cut one edge of the pittas open and fill with ingredients of your choice. Put any leftover bread in the freezer.

MAKES 20
25g/1oz fresh yeast
3½ tbsp olive oil
500ml/17fl oz/generous 2 cups water
about 600g/1lb 5oz/ plain flour, plus
  extra for dusting
1 tsp salt
1 tsp sugar

BEETROOT RISOTTO
WITH TOASTED ALMONDS & GOAT'S CHEESE CREAM

This is the dish that makes frightened children burst out with 'you're eating raw mince!'. In our opinion, it's both beautiful and incredible tasty. Risotto is a vegetarian classic that can be varied in many ways. The base is made out of rice that's cooked with stock, white wine and cheese until creamy. Then you can flavour the risotto with whatever you fancy: chanterelles, asparagus, roasted tomatoes or green beans. No matter what you choose it's a good idea to garnish the whole thing with toasted almonds and croûtons for added crunch.

1. Heat the oil in a pan and quickly sauté the shallots and garlic until soft, then add the grated beetroot and the rice.
2. Add the wine and bring to the boil, stirring. Then pour in the stock and about 100ml/3½fl oz/scant ½ cup of the water and continue to stir until the liquid has been absorbed. Continue to add water a little at a time, allowing it to cook into the rice.
3. Meanwhile, mix together the crumbled goat's cheese and yogurt for the topping.
4. Heat up a dry frying pan and toast the almonds.
5. When the rice has softened, stir in the grated cheese. Season to taste with salt and pepper, if needed.
6. Serve the risotto with almonds, goat's cheese cream, croûtons and a salad.

SERVES 4

2 tbsp rapeseed or olive oil
3–4 shallots, chopped
3 garlic cloves, chopped
4 beetroots (about 300g/10½oz), coarsely grated
260g/9¼oz/scant 1¼ cups arborio rice or other risotto rice
200ml/7fl oz/scant 1 cup white wine
2 tbsp concentrated liquid vegetable stock
700ml/24fl oz/3 cups water
100g/3½oz/1¼ cups Parmesan cheese, freshly grated
salt and freshly ground black pepper

To serve
100g/3½oz goat's cheese, crumbled
100g/3½oz/generous ⅓ cup thick yogurt (10% fat)
120g/4¼oz/heaped 1 cup coarsely chopped almonds
50g/2oz croûtons (buy ready-made or roast bread cubes with oil and salt in the oven)
fresh green salad

LASAGNE
WITH HAZELNUT PASTE & MUSHROOMS

It's unclear why this lasagne feels so luxurious, but it does. Perhaps it's something to do with the nutty flavour? Or simply because it's just so incredibly delicious.

1. Preheat the oven to 220°C/425°F/gas 7 or the temperature advised on the lasagne sheet packet.
2. Toast the hazelnuts in a dry, hot frying pan. Reserve a handful for the garnish, then tip them into a bowl and add the cottage cheese and parsley and blend into a smooth paste using a stick blender.
3. Fry the aubergines and mushrooms in the butter with the garlic until soft and most of the liquid has evaporated. Sprinkle with salt and pepper.
4. Melt the butter for the béchamel sauce in a pan and stir in the flour. Whisk in the milk a little at a time and bring to the boil. Add the stock cube or concentrated liquid stock. Simmer, whisking constantly, for 3 minutes until the sauce has thickened.
5. Layer the béchamel sauce, lasagne sheets, hazelnut paste and the mushroom and aubergine mixture in an ovenproof dish: start with a layer of béchamel sauce in the bottom and finish with a layer of hazelnut cream and béchamel sauce on top. This means it's important to make sure you've got enough sauce and hazelnut paste left to spread out on the top of the lasagne.
6. Sprinkle over the grated cheese and garnish with the reserved hazelnuts. Bake in the oven according to the instructions on the lasagne sheet packet.

SERVES 4

120g/4¼oz/1 cup hazelnuts (can be replaced with almonds or sunflower seeds)
500g/1lb 2oz cottage cheese
2 handfuls of parsley leaves
1 large or 2 small aubergines, chopped or thinly sliced
225g/8oz/3¾ cups mushrooms (can be replaced with other types of mushroom), chopped or thinly sliced
3 tbsp butter
2 garlic cloves
85g/3oz/scant 1 cup hard cheese, grated
about 10 lasagne sheets (dried)
salt and freshly ground black pepper

Béchamel sauce
2 tbsp butter
4 tbsp plain flour
700ml/24fl oz/3 cups milk
1 vegetable stock cube or 1 tbsp concentrated liquid vegetable stock

To serve
a colourful mixed salad

FRESH SPRING ROLLS
WITH PEANUT DIP

Yes, it's a bit fiddly to prepare fresh spring rolls until you get the hang of it. And yes, it looks a bit like you're cooking food in rubber. But it's worth it, because these rolls are extremely delicious.

1. Place a rice paper in tepid water for 15 seconds or as long as indicated on the packet instructions. Repeat with the rest of the rice papers and space out on a clean dish cloth.
2. Place some carrot, avocado, tofu, spring onion, nuts, bean sprouts and coriander leaves in a rectangular pile across the middle of each rice paper. Wrap the rolls according to the packet instructions.
2. Mix together the peanut butter and hot water in a bowl. Add the sweet chilli sauce, soy sauce and sesame oil. Drizzle a little of this sauce over the rolls and serve the rest separately.

> **TIP!**
> An alternative filling is stir-fried carrot, leek, bean sprouts, cashew nuts, coriander and cooked cellophane noodles with a dash of hoisin sauce and grated fresh root ginger. This will make the spring rolls feel more cooked and spicy.

SERVES 4 (ABOUT 16 ROLLS)

Rolls

about 16 rice papers (you'll find these in larger supermarkets or Asian food stores)

1–2 carrots, peeled and thinly sliced

3 avocados, peeled, pitted and sliced

400g/14oz tofu, natural or marinated, sliced

7 spring onions, sliced

180g/6¼oz/1½ cups cashew nuts, coarsely chopped

150g/5½oz bean sprouts (fresh or tinned)

2 handfuls of coriander leaves

Dipping sauce

45g/1½ oz/⅓ cup peanut butter

3½ tbsp hot water

3½ tbsp sweet chilli sauce

2 tbsp Japanese soy sauce

1 tbsp sesame oil

TACO BURGERS

A burger with taco flavour – the best of both worlds? The trickiest thing with vegetarian patties and burgers is to get them to hold together in the frying pan when you're flipping them over. You often find yourself standing by the cooker, cursing the mixture that breaks apart in front of your eyes as you see your perfectly formed patties turn into mulch. But these burgers are beautifully easy to handle! The base is made from tofu and beans, so with just a few barely noticeable adjustments this is a burger that would also appeal to vegans.

1. Mix the garlic and soured cream to make a dressing. (Or use a dollop of aioli or guacamole as a dressing instead – also delicious!)
2. Blend together the beans, taco spice mix and pepper, this is easiest if you use a hand-held mixer and a bowl. Mash up the tofu with a fork and stir into the paste – it's better if the paste isn't completely smooth.
3. Crush the tortilla chips, not too coarsely, and add half to the burger mixture with the flour. Divide the mixture into 4–6 patties and press together firmly so they hold their shape. Turn them over in the rest of the tortilla crumbs, as a coating.
4. Fry the burgers for a couple of minutes on each side in a generous splash of oil. Serve them in hamburger buns with the dressing and other toppings.

Choose vegan-friendly tortilla crisps. Use a spoonful of classic taco salsa as dressing for the burger.

SERVES 4

Patties

400g/14oz tin kidney beans, drained and rinsed

4 tbsp Taco Spice Mix (see below)

1 pinch of freshly ground black pepper

300g/10½oz firm tofu, natural or marinated

1 cup crushed tortilla chips, preferably with a cheesy flavour

4 tbsp plain flour

rapeseed oil, for frying

To serve

1 small garlic clove, crushed

200ml/7fl oz/scant 1 cup soured cream

4 hamburger rolls

1 red onion, sliced

1–2 avocados, peeled, pitted and sliced

1 red pepper, deseeded and sliced

115g/4oz/scant 1 cup sweetcorn

a few large lettuce or fresh spinach leaves

TACO SPICE MIX
It's easy to make your own taco spice mix. Mix together 1 tbsp chilli powder, 1 tbsp onion powder, 1 tbsp ground cumin, 1 tsp paprika, 1 tsp dried oregano, 1 tsp sugar, 1 tsp salt and ¼ tsp black pepper. Keep in a screw-top jar.

SUMPTUOUS CHILLI
WITH CHOCOLATE

'Sumptuous' might not be a word that's often heard in the same sentence as 'vegetarian', but this chilli really is that, as well as filling and flavourful. The smoky flavour comes from chipotle paste. Chipotle is basically smoked chilli, and you'll find chipotle chilli paste in a jar among other spices and sauces in the supermarket. Check out the store's Tex-Mex shelf, if they have one.

1. Sweat the onion, garlic and chilli – with or without the seeds, depending on how hot you like it – in a little oil in a medium-hot heavy-based pan for a few minutes.
2. Add the cumin, thyme, oregano and paprika and stir for another minute.
3. Add the wine, soy sauce, chipotle paste and chopped tomatoes and leave to simmer gently for quite a while, covered with a lid, preferably for 40 minutes.
4. Once the 40 minutes have passed, throw in the carrot first, followed by the peppers, courgette and beans. Leave to simmer until everything has got the right texture, about 15–20 minutes. Dilute with water if needed, but don't add too much! The chilli should be quite thick.
5. Stir in the chocolate. Season to taste with salt and pepper. Sprinkle over the parsley and serve with bread, preferably topped with cream cheese – it's so nice with chilli!

Choose a dairy-free chocolate and skip the cream cheese.

SERVES 4

1 onion, chopped

3 garlic cloves, chopped

1 red chilli, deseeded and chopped

3 tbsp olive oil

2 tbsp ground cumin

1 tbsp dried thyme

1 tbsp dried oregano

1 tbsp ground paprika

about 300ml/½ pint/1¼ cups full-bodied red wine

1 tbsp Chinese soy sauce

1 tsp chipotle chilli paste

500g/1lb 2oz tinned chopped tomatoes

1 carrot, peeled and chopped

2 small peppers, preferably in different colours, deseeded and cut into chunks

1 courgette, cut into chunks

400g/14oz tin chickpeas or borlotti beans, drained

400g/14oz tin kidney beans, drained

about 240ml/8fl oz/1 cup water (you might not need this)

20g/½ oz dark chocolate, grated or broken into pieces

salt and freshly ground black pepper

25g/1oz chopped parsley leaves

<u>To serve</u>
bread and cream cheese

VEGETARIAN DUMPLINGS

WITH CELLOPHANE NOODLE SALAD

It's really not difficult to make your own dumplings. Here we've taken a shortcut and bought ready-made dumpling cases, to invest our energy into making two different dipping sauces instead. But, of course, you can make your own dough, too, if you've plenty of time! Remember to chop the dumpling filling finely, and it will be easier to get nice even parcels.

1. Start by making the dipping sauces: stir together the ingredients for each sauce.
2. Prepare the noodles according to the instructions on the packet.
3. Mix the garlic with soy sauce, oil and lime juice. Add the vegetables and stir-fry them quickly, then mix them together with the noodles and dressing. This is best served cold.
4. For the dumplings, heat a dash of oil in a stir-fry pan and stir-fry all the vegetables thoroughly, so that they starts to colour and cook together into a nice filling. Add soy sauce to taste.
5. Place 1½ tbsp filling onto each dumpling wrapper, wet the edge of the circle with some water, fold and press so that the edges stick together properly.
6. Sauté a few dumplings at a time in oil in a stir-fry pan. Don't fry all of them at once if there's not enough space. Stir so that they all crisp up on the outside. Pour over 3½ tbsp water, put the lid on top if you've got one and leave them to steam for about a minute, before serving with the noodle salad and dipping sauces.

 Replace soured cream with a soya alternative.

SERVES 4

Dipping sauce with chilli & peanut

2 tbsp peanut butter
100ml/3½fl oz/½ cup soured cream
2 tbsp sweet chilli sauce
1 tbsp Japanese soy sauce

Dipping sauce with prune & ginger

125g/4½oz prune purée (1 baby food jar)
1 tbsp Japanese soy sauce
1–2 pinches of ground ginger

Cellophane noodle salad

100g/3½oz cellophane noodles
1 garlic clove, chopped
3 tbsp Japanese soy sauce
1 tbsp rapeseed oil
1½ tbsp freshly squeezed lime juice (1–2 limes)
150g/5½oz/1½ cups mangetout, chopped
1 red pepper, deseeded and chopped
½ small sweetheart or white cabbage, shredded

Dumplings

rapeseed oil, for frying
1 onion, chopped
2 garlic cloves, chopped
1–2 tbsp chopped fresh root ginger
1 carrot, peeled and coarsely grated
1 pepper, deseeded and chopped
1 aubergine, diced
75g/2½oz soya beans
100g/3½oz kale, cavolo nero or white cabbage, finely shredded
2 tbsp light Japanese soy sauce
30–40 defrosted dumpling or wonton wrappers

POTATO TART
WITH TRUFFLE SAUCE

With a crispy bottom of puff pasty, this potato dish feels even more decadent than a sweet tart. And it looks beautiful too!

1. Preheat the oven to 200°C/400°F/gas 6.
2. Wash the potatoes and boil in the skins until just soft. Drain, cool, then cut into 1.5cm/⅝in slices.
3. Trim the asparagus and cut into 3cm/1½in pieces. Sweat in oil with the onion and garlic until soft.
4. Grease a tart dish and arrange the potato slices attractively in the dish, cut sides down. You will flip the tart over eventually, so the base will be on show! Put the asparagus, onion and sundried tomatoes on top and push them gently into the gaps in between the potato circles as much as you can.
5. Dollop cream cheese on top of the tart and sprinkle over some oregano. If the sundried tomatoes came in a lovely marinade it's a good idea to tip some of that over the filling too, for extra flavour.
6. Roll out the puff pastry sheets and place them over the filling in the tart dish. Place one of the sheets to cover half of the dish and the other to cover the rest. Fold the edges of the pastry down in between the filling and the dish, as if you were folding in a blanket. Bake in the oven according to the instructions on the puff pastry packet, until the pastry is golden and cooked through.
7. Meanwhile, make the sauce. Fry the shallots until soft. Add the crème fraîche and 100ml/3½fl oz/scant ½ cup water and bring to the boil. Leave to simmer gently, stirring continuously, for about a minute, then add more stock and truffle oil or paste to taste.
8. Take out the tart from the oven and leave to cool for a few minutes. Then flip it upside down with the help from a large plate or a tray. If a potato piece comes loose during the flipping it's no big deal, it's easy to 'repair' the tart afterwards. Garnish with fresh oregano. Serve with salad and bread.

SERVES 4

Potato tart
1kg/2lb 4oz baby potatoes
250g/9oz green asparagus
1 onion, sliced into rings
1 garlic clove, chopped
rapeseed or olive oil, for frying
8 marinated sundried tomatoes
150g/5½oz cream cheese
1 handful of oregano leaves
salt and freshly ground black
* pepper*
2 puff pastry sheets

Truffle sauce
2 shallots, chopped
200ml/7fl oz/scant 1 cup crème
* fraîche*
1–2 tsp concentrated liquid
* vegetable stock or ½ vegetable*
* stock cube*
truffle oil or truffle paste, to taste

To serve
salad and bread

CANNELLONI
WITH WINTER CHANTERELLES & CHEESE

*I dream about these pasta rolls – I wake suddenly
in the middle of the night, sit up in bed and, like
a drowsy Homer Simpson, have thoughts along the
lines of 'mmm… winter chanterelles'. They are
very scrumptious.*

1. Start by making the tomato sauce. Sweat the
   garlic in a dash of oil in a pan. Add the tomato
   purée and fry for another minute. Add the rest of
   the ingredients for the sauce (except the salt and
   pepper) and leave to simmer into a tasty sauce
   while you prepare the rest of the dish. Season to
   taste with salt and pepper.
2. Fry all the mushrooms in the butter on a low heat
   in a large frying pan.
3. Add the onion and carrots and stir in, then add the
   garlic and fry for another minute. Season to taste
   with salt and pepper.
4. Remove the pan from the heat and stir in the
   cottage cheese and thyme.
5. Put a dollop of filling the size of about 3 tbsp onto
   one of the short edges of a lasagne sheet and roll
   into a tube. Place the tube in an ovenproof dish,
   with the seam facing down. Continue until you're
   out of lasagne sheets and filling.
6. Pour the tomato sauce over the rolls and top with
   the grated cheese.
7. Bake in the oven according to the instructions
   on the lasagne sheet packet, about 20 minutes.
   Garnish with thyme and serve with a mixed salad.

SERVES 4

Tomato sauce
1 garlic clove, chopped
olive oil
1 tbsp tomato purée
400g/14oz tin chopped tomatoes
1 tsp granulated sugar
1 vegetable stock cube
2 tbsp balsamic vinegar
*salt and freshly ground black
    pepper*

Rolls
*450g/1lb fresh winter chanterelles,
    chopped*
225g/8oz fresh mushrooms, chopped
25g/1oz butter
1 onion, finely chopped
*2 large carrots, peeled and coarsely
    grated*
1 garlic clove, chopped
*salt and freshly ground black
    pepper*
500g/1lb 2oz cottage cheese
*1 small handful of thyme leaves,
    plus extra to garnish*
8–12 fresh lasagne sheets
100g/3½oz Swiss cheese, grated

To serve
a mixed salad

MEZE

The concept of having lots of small dishes, where everyone can serve themselves their favourites, really is a blessing for family dinners where everyone prefers different things. Here's our loose interpretation of some vegetarian meze dishes.

TABBOULEH WITH POMEGRANATE

Fresh tomatoes feature in a traditional tabbouleh, but we've swapped them for pomegranate seeds. This dish tastes better if it's prepared a while in advance, so that the bulgur has time to soak up the flavours.

SERVES 4

160g/5½oz/scant 1 cup bulgur wheat
400ml/14fl oz/1¾ cups water or tomato juice
1 pinch of salt
1 onion, chopped
1 garlic clove, chopped
100g/3½oz/2 cups finely chopped parsley leaves
juice of 1 lemon or 2 limes
3½ tbsp olive oil
1 pomegranate
salt and freshly ground black pepper

1. Boil the bulgur in the water or in tomato juice with the salt, following the instructions on the packet. Drain and leave to cool.
2. Mix the onion, garlic and parsley with the lemon or lime juice and the olive oil.
3. Mix in the cooled bulgur and pomegranate seeds. Season to taste and add more lemon or lime juice, if needed.

GARLIC-SCENTED ARTICHOKE DIP

SERVES 4

400g/14oz tin artichokes, drained and cut into chunks
2 garlic cloves, chopped
3½ tbsp olive oil, plus extra for frying
200g/7oz/scant 1 cup cooked or tinned butter beans
salt and freshly ground black pepper
paprika
juice of 1 lemon

1. Sweat the artichokes and garlic quickly together in a dash of oil in a frying pan.
2. Place the artichoke mixture in a bowl with the beans and blend until smooth using a stick blender.
3. Stir in the olive oil and add salt, pepper, paprika and lemon juice to taste.

YOGURT SAUCE WITH MINT

SERVES 4

200g/7oz/scant 1 cup thick yogurt (10% fat)
2–3 tbsp finely chopped mint leaves
juice of 1 lemon
olive oil (optional)
salt and freshly ground black pepper

1. Mix together the yogurt and mint.
2. Season with salt and pepper and add a dash of lemon juice and olive oil, if using.

More recipes overleaf ››

BAKED MINI PEPPERS WITH CREAM CHEESE

MAKES ABOUT 8

55g/2oz marinated sundried tomatoes, chopped
55g/2oz/½ cup pitted black olives
1 garlic clove, chopped
200g/7oz natural cream cheese
1–2 tsp dried thyme
½ pinch of white pepper
4–5 small colourful peppers, cored

1. Preheat the oven to 220°C/425°F/gas 7.
2. Mix the tomatoes, olives and garlic, then stir in the cream cheese, herbs and spices.
3. Fill the peppers with the mixture and bake in the oven for 10–15 minutes or until they've coloured nicely.

CRISPY CHEESE ROLLS

MAKES 16

300g/10½oz feta cheese
3 tbsp chopped mint leaves
3 tbsp chopped fresh parsley leaves
2 pinches of white pepper
½ pinch of chilli flakes (optional)
16 filo pastry sheets (25 x 35cm/10 x 14in)
olive oil, for brushing

1. Preheat the oven to 220°C/425°F/gas 7.
2. Crumble the cheese into a bowl. Add the herbs and spices and stir.
3. Spread out the filling at the bottom of the short edge of each filo sheet. Fold in the edges and roll together.
4. Brush with olive oil and bake in the middle of the oven for 10–15 minutes, or until the rolls are golden brown.
5. Pitta bread is, of course, also nice served with meze!

Fancy baking your own pitta breads? Check out the recipe on page 100!

TEX-MEX PLATTER

Some like it hot, others don't. But everyone likes Tex-Mex. Try gradually adding the chilli to the salsa, chilli butter and quesadillas, so you don't traumatize anyone around the table.

MANGO SALSA WITH BOURBON, CHILLI & CORIANDER

This salsa is flavoured with bourbon (American whisky), but you can leave this out if you prefer.

SERVES 4

1 mango
1 small red onion, finely chopped
1 red or green chilli, deseeded and finely
  chopped
1 tsp granulated sugar
1 tbsp bourbon (optional)
chopped coriander leaves
salt and freshly ground black pepper

1. Peel, pit and chop the mango.
2. Mix all the ingredients except the salt and pepper in a bowl. Add the chilli and the coriander gradually so you can include exactly how much you prefer. Season to taste with salt and pepper.

CRISPY ONION RINGS

SERVES 4

40g/1½oz/¾ cup panko breadcrumbs (can be
  replaced with standard breadcrumbs)
1 tsp salt flakes
1 tsp dried chilli flakes
55g/2oz/scant ½ cup plain flour
1 egg, lightly beaten
1 onion, sliced into rings
rapeseed oil, for frying

1. Mix the panko with the salt and chilli on a deep plate.
2. Put the flour on a second plate and the egg in another.
3. Dip the onion rings in the flour first, then in the egg and finally in the panko mixture.
4. Heat up a generous amount of rapeseed oil in a frying pan and fry the onion rings in the oil until they've turned golden.

More recipes overleaf »

GRILLED CORN ON THE COB WITH LIME & CHILLI BUTTER

SERVES 4

1 chilli pepper, deseeded and finely chopped
grated zest of 1 lime
90g/3oz butter, softened
4 parboiled corn on the cobs

1. Mix together the chilli and lime zest.
2. Blend into the butter, adding the flavourings gradually so you can adjust them to your taste.
3. Grill the corn cobs until tender, basting with the spiced butter as they cook.

 Replace the butter with dairy-free spread.

BEAN & PEPPER-FILLED QUESADILLAS

SERVES 4

400g/14oz tin kidney beans, drained and rinsed
½ onion, finely chopped
1 red pepper, deseeded and finely chopped
55g/2oz/½ cup sweetcorn
100ml/3½fl oz/scant ½ cup taco sauce
1 handful of coriander leaves, finely chopped
8 wheat tortillas
110g/3¾oz1¼ cups grated cheese
rapeseed oil, for frying

1. Blend the kidney beans until chunky using a stick blender, then stir in the onion, pepper, sweetcorn, taco sauce and coriander.
2. Spread out the filling onto a tortilla and sprinkle with a generous amount of cheese, then place another tortilla on top as a lid.
3. Heat a little oil and fry the whole thing in a frying pan for about a minute on each side until it has turned golden and the cheese has melted.
4. Cut into triangles and serve.

PAD THAI
WITH CRISPY TOFU

The trick to getting the tofu really crispy in this dish is to roll it in cornflour before frying it. It makes an enormous difference!

1. Mix together the soy sauce, lime juice and sugar.
2. Save some spring onion for garnishing. Sauté the remainder with the carrots and garlic in a hot stir-fry pan until coloured and starting to soften. Add the bean sprouts and fry for a little longer.
3. Boil the rice noodles for 3 minutes in salted water. Drain, cover with cold water and leave to rest.
4. Make some space in the stir-fry pan, for frying the eggs. Crack one in at a time, leave until they start to set and then stir. Add the drained noodles, a little at a time, and mix together as best you can. Add the soy-lime-sugar sauce and keep on stir-frying until everything is mixed together.
5. Mix together the cornflour, chilli and salt in a bowl, dice the tofu and roll it around in the mixture. Fry the tofu in a separate pan in a generous amount of oil until the tofu has coloured somewhat. Stir into the noodle mixture. Sprinkle over the remaining spring onion and some of the peanuts and serve with the remaining peanuts offered separately.

 Leave out the eggs.

SERVES 4

4 tbsp Japanese soy sauce
juice from 1–2 limes (2–3 tbsp in total)
2 tbsp sugar
about 7 spring onions, sliced
3 carrots, peeled and sliced
3 garlic cloves, chopped
rapeseed oil, for frying
150g/5½oz fresh bean sprouts
200g/7oz flat rice noodles
3 eggs
45g/1½oz/heaped ⅓ cup cornflour (or potato flour)
½ tsp chilli flakes
½ tsp salt
300g/10½oz firm tofu
200g/7oz/1½ cups peanuts, chopped

<u>*To serve*</u>
more lime juice, peanuts, soy sauce, chilli and coriander

TORTELLINI
WITH ROASTED PEPPER SAUCE

*You can make your own tortellini if you want, but
it is time-consuming and fiddly. Here we've bought
ready-made, fresh tortellini. Often there are several
different vegetarian flavours to choose from, like
mushroom, cheese or spinach. If you can find some
with a ricotta filling, they go well with this sauce.*

1. Preheat the oven to 250°C/500°F/gas 9.
2. Put the peppers, cut-side down, in a roasting pan.
   Grill them until they start getting black spots and
   the skin starts to get bubbly – about 10 minutes.
   The timing can vary from oven to oven, so keep an
   eye on the peppers, but don't be afraid to let them
   get quite dark, so it's easy to peel them afterwards.
3. Leave the peppers to cool, then pull off the skins.
   It doesn't matter if there's still some skin left on
   if it gets too fiddly.
4. Sweat the shallots and garlic in a little oil in a
   pan. Add the peppers, cream, wine and stock cube
   and leave to simmer for a couple of minutes. Blend
   the sauce until smooth, using a stick blender.
5. Add pepper and thyme to taste.
6. Meanwhile, cook the tortellini according to the
   instructions on the packet and serve immediately
   with the sauce poured over the top.

Replace the cream with a soya
or oat alternative and serve
with egg-free pasta.

SERVES 4
5 red peppers, halved and deseeded
3 shallots, chopped
1–2 garlic cloves, chopped
olive oil
5 tbsp cream
5 tbsp white wine
1 stock cube
freshly ground black pepper and
   fresh thyme, to taste
500–600g/1lb 2oz–1lb 5oz fresh
   tortellini

VEGGIE FOOD
for
THE BABY

If you want to feed your child
solely on vegetarian food, ask
your child's health visitor or
GP for more detailed advice.

It's absolutely fine to give vegetarian food to really small children too, and here pretty much the same basic rules apply as for when you cook baby food containing meat: boil and mash – or serve soft pieces when the baby can cope with them.

quick fixes!

a complete veggie meal for a baby contains:

A source of protein, such as red lentils, mung beans, chickpeas, tofu or egg – these are foods that don't only contain protein, but also vitamins and minerals; a source of carbohydrates, such as pasta, potato, couscous or root vegetables; one or several vegetables; a dash of rapeseed oil, which contains the vital fatty acids omega-3 and omega-6 and which the body can't produce on its own; a drink, for example breast milk, follow-on milk or water; and preferably fruit or berries for dessert – this will help the baby to take up the iron in the food more efficiently.

Sometimes (quite often) the baby is hungry NOW! What can you do? Avocado is a perfect snack – just mash up and feed.

Cooked or tinned pulses like chickpeas, kidney beans, black eye beans and lentils are also good to take out and mash with some oil or pesto.

Tofu doesn't have to be cooked, but can be given to the baby as it is.

Green peas can be blended into a pea purée in the blink of an eye. Or into a creamy soup with avocado, some hot water, garlic and a nice herb.

Scrambled eggs – very simple and nutritious.

But the easiest, and perhaps the most fun: the food that the rest of the family eats! Most of it can safely be given to babies from six months old – in the right consistency and as long as it's not too salty. Try Pasta Rosso (page 37), Red Lentil and Coconut Curry (page 78) or Creamy Three-bean Masala (page 60).

SNACKS & SWEETS

There are occasions when it doesn't feel quite right to place a cast-iron pot with a warming slow-cooked creation on the table. Snack-time is one example. When it's time for an aperitif, another. Not to mention dessert – yes, good grief, people could actually think you've lost your mind if you came in with a lentil curry on those occasions! This is nothing to worry about. You've still got the following chapter to go. Everything will be okay.

DEEP-FRIED AVOCADO
WITH LIME AIOLI

It might sound strange to deep-fry avocado and eat it warm, but it's worth trying. Especially if you've got avocados at home that aren't soft enough to eat as they are, and if you can't face waiting until they've ripened properly. Very tasty, very filling, and bordering on addictive.

DEEP-FRIED AVOCADO

1. Mix the flour and salt together on a plate.
2. Beat the egg yolks with a fork on a deep plate.
3. Place the panko on a third plate.
4. Cut the avocados into chunks and dip each chunk first into the flour, then in the egg and finally in the panko and then deep-fry gently or pan-fry in oil until golden and crispy. (For the latter method you won't need as much oil.) Drain on a piece of kitchen paper and serve with lime aioli.

LIME AIOLI

1. Mix together the egg yolks, vinegar and mustard in a steady bowl, preferably so heavy that you don't have to hold it while whisking.
2. Pour the oil into a jug or similar and add very slowly to the egg mixture, while also whisking vigorously until the aioli thickens.
3. Add garlic and lime juice to taste.

SERVES 4
Deep-fried avocado
55g/2oz/scant ½ cup plain flour
½ tsp herb seasoning salt (or regular salt)
1–2 eggs
80g/2¾/1 cup panko breadcrumbs (can be replaced with standard breadcrumbs)
2 avocados (preferably too hard rather than too soft)
olive oil, for deep frying

MAKES 300ml/½ pint/1¼ cups
Lime aioli
2 egg yolks
1 tbsp white wine vinegar
1 tsp Dijon mustard
250ml/9fl oz/generous 1 cup rapeseed oil
1 garlic clove
juice from 1 lime

ICE LOLLIES

Making your own ice lollies from fruit and berries is ridiculously simple. And once you've started trying out different flavour combinations, it's hard to stop. If you can't find ice lolly moulds in your local store, search for them online. The simple syrup is used as a base for all the ice lolly recipes.

SIMPLE SYRUP
FOR 10 ICE LOLLIES YOU'LL NEED:
200ml/7fl oz/scant 1 cup water
200g/7oz/1 cup granulated sugar

1. Bring the water and sugar to the boil in pan and leave to simmer until the sugar has dissolved.
2. Remove the pan from the heat. Add any spices that are used in your chosen ice lolly recipe. Leave to cool.

RASPBERRY & CREAM LOLLIES
MAKES 10 ICE LOLLIES
500g/1lb 2oz raspberries
200ml/7fl oz/scant 1 cup Simple Syrup
120ml/4fl oz/½ cup double or whipping cream

1. Place the raspberries in a bowl and blend with a stick blender.
2. Add half of the simple syrup and stir thoroughly. Check the flavour. You might not need to add all of the syrup. Add until you think it's sweet enough!
3. Add the un-whipped cream and stir just a little bit – it's nice if you've got some ripples running through as this will make the lollies look extra pretty.
4. Pour the raspberry mixture into your ice lolly moulds and leave to stand in the freezer for 4–5 hours.

BLUEBERRY & CARDAMOM LOLLIES
MAKES 10 ICE LOLLIES
500g/1lb 2oz blueberries
200ml/7fl oz/scant 1 cup Simple Syrup
2 tsp fresh lemon juice
1–2 pinches ground cardamom (that you stir into the Simple Syrup when making it)

1. Place the blueberries in a bowl and blend them using a stick blender.
2. Add half of the simple syrup and stir thoroughly. Check the flavour. You might not need to add all of the syrup. Add until you think it's sweet enough!
3. Pour the blueberry mixture into your ice lolly moulds and leave to stand in the freezer for 4–5 hours.

MANGO & ELDERFLOWER LOLLIES
MAKES 10 ICE LOLLIES
500g/1lb 2oz diced mango (frozen is fine!)
3½ tbsp concentrated elderflower cordial
150ml/¼ pint/scant ⅔ cup Simple Syrup

1. Put the mango pieces into a bowl and blend them using a stick blender.
2. Add the elderflower cordial and some of the simple syrup. Check the flavour! It's very likely that you might not need to add all of the syrup. Add until you think it's sweet enough!
3. Pour the mango mixture into your ice lolly moulds and leave to stand in the freezer for 4–5 hours.

 Replace the cream in the raspberry ice lollies with an oat or soya alternative.

TIP!
Save leftover slush in the
freezer and take out, leave
to defrost a little and serve
as a sorbet.

SMOOTHIES

Taking out the stick blender and letting yourself loose among fruit and berries is a simple way to fix a good snack. And it also opens up endless possibilities to 'hide' healthy stuff under a colourful surface. If you want to deceive someone who's afraid of the healthy stuff, smoothies are for you!

SMOOTHIE WITH BLUEBERRIES
When the fruit in the fruit bowl starts to look depressed it's time to make it into a smoothie. The pear on the edge of over-ripeness used here makes this yogurt drink taste delicious.

SERVES 2
100g/3½oz blueberries
1 very ripe pear
100g/3½oz/scant ½ cup yogurt
100ml/3½fl oz/scant ½ cup milk or more
½ avocado (optional, but is very good to make the smoothie filling)
some juice from a lime

1. Blend everything. Add more milk until you've got a good consistency and add lime juice to taste.

 Replace the yogurt and milk in the smoothie with an oat or soya alternative.

ORANGE & PEACH SMOOTHIE
Apart from the fact that the combination of sour orange and sweet peach is very tasty, this smoothie is a proper vitamin bomb, packed with vitamin C.

SERVES 2
3 oranges
2 peaches
1 passion fruit

1. Peel the oranges, peel and stone the peaches and scrape out the seeds and pulp from the passion fruit. Blitz in a blender or juicer and serve.

STRAWBERRY SLUSHIE WITH ELDERFLOWER & LEMON
An insanely delicious drink that takes only 2 minutes to prepare. You'll also get folic acid, iron and magnesium as a bonus.

SERVES 2
300ml/½ pint/1¼ cups diluted elderflower cordial, preferably quite concentrated
250g/9oz frozen strawberries
3 ice cubes
some freshly squeezed lemon juice
a sprig of lemon balm (optional)

1. Put the cordial and strawberries into a deep bowl and blend until smooth. Add the ice cubes and continue blending.
2. Add lemon juice to taste and garnish with a sprig of lemon balm.

WHAT IS CARRAGEENAN?
There are several alternative jellifying substances for those who don't want to use gelatine (which comes from animals), for example, agar agar, pectin or gelling sugar. Here we've used carrageenan iota, which needs to be heated before it's added to your recipe. It's completely vegetarian, as it's made from a red algae. You'll find it in specialist food stores.

Honestly speaking, the first time we heard about chocolate mousse made from avocado we thought it sounded rather nasty. But try it! Especially if you've got an avocado at home that's tipped over the verge of ultimate ripeness. Then it's perfect for transforming into a dessert. The result is a smooth and creamy mousse, without a single dairy product in sight, that takes 5 minutes to prepare.

If you want, you can flavour the chocolate mousse with vanilla, cinnamon or cardamom. But it's not at all necessary – it's lovely just as it is.

PANNACOTTA
WITH CARDAMOM & PASSION FRUIT

Normally pannacotta contains gelatine, but since gelatine is an animal-based product, we've replaced it with carrageenan (see left). You can vary the flavourings. Try replacing the cardamom with cinnamon or saffron, and garnish with sliced apple or pomegranate seeds.

1. Mix the together cream, sugar and cardamom in a pan and bring to the boil.
2. Remove from the heat immediately and leave aside.
3. Mix the carrageenan and water in another pan and bring to the boil for 30 seconds, whisking constantly.
4. Add the cream mixture and whisk everything until smooth. Pour into small glasses or cups. Leave to set in the fridge for at least 1 hour.
5. Scrape out the seeds and pulp from the passion fruits and layer on top of the pannacotta. Garnish with lemon balm, if you want, and serve.

SERVES 4–6
300ml/½ pint/1¼ cups cream
4 tbsp granulated sugar
1–2 pinches of ground cardamom
4 pinches of carrageenan iota
3½ tbsp water
3 passion fruits
a few leaves of lemon balm (optional)

CHOCOLATE MOUSSE
WITH AVOCADO

1. Scrape out the flesh from the avocados and place in a small deep bowl with the dates, cocoa powder, water and honey.
2. Blend to a smooth mousse with a dash of lemon juice. Garnish with berries and mint.

 Replace the honey with maple syrup.

SERVES 4
3 ripe avocados (better too soft than too hard)
10 pitted dates
65g/2¼oz/⅔ cup cocoa powder
3½ tbsp water
about 2 tbsp clear honey (honey should not be given to children under 1 year old)
freshly squeezed lemon juice (optional)
berries to serve
mint sprig, to garnish

HEALTHY TREATS

SNACK MUFFINS WITH CARROT & CINNAMON

These muffins fall somewhere between wholesome and healthy snacks and delicious cakes, so you can happily eat them at snack times without thinking twice. The carrot can be replaced with grated pear, apple or mashed banana if you want to vary the flavour, and you can replace the porridge oats with muesli. And if there are any muffins left over, you can put them in the freezer.

MAKES 18

235g/8½oz/scant 2 cups plain flour
90g/3oz/1 cup oat bran or porridge oats
1 pinch of salt
2 tsp baking powder
1 tbsp ground cinnamon
50g/1¾oz/¼ cup demerara sugar, or granulated sugar
3–4 carrots, peeled and finely grated
150ml/¼ pint/scant ⅔ cup rapeseed oil
200g/7oz/scant 1 cup plain yogurt
2 eggs

1. Preheat the oven to 200°C/400°C/gas 6.
2. Mix the flour, oat bran, salt, baking powder, cinnamon and sugar in a bowl.
3. Add the carrots with the oil, yogurt and eggs and mix to a smooth batter. Spoon into muffin cases.
4. Bake in the middle of the oven for about 20 minutes or until the muffins have coloured nicely. Serve as they are or with butter and cheese.

POWERBALLS WITH DATES & CHOCOLATE

These may look similar to standard chocolate balls, but on the inside they are a lot healthier. That is, they contain more seeds and fruits and less refined sugar.

MAKES ABOUT 30 BALLS

200g/7oz/heaped 1½ cups pitted dates
5 tbsp rapeseed oil
70g/2½oz/½ cup sunflower seeds
70g/2½oz/½ cup sesame seeds
2 tbsp cocoa powder
95g/3¼oz/1 cup porridge oats
3 tbsp desiccated coconut, plus extra for coating the balls

1. Blend the dates and oil in a food processor or using a stick blender. Add the rest of the ingredients and continue to blend until everything is mixed.
2. Form into balls or bars and coat in coconut. Store in a cool, dry place.

More recipes overleaf »

FLAPJACKS WITH PAPAYA & CASHEW NUTS

Flapjack is a fancy name for a decently wholesome oat cake filled with tasty things. You bake it in a deep roasting pan, pack it full of nuts and seeds and fruit and then cut it into bars. Then you serve the flapjacks as a snack and think things like 'oh, well – at least it's better than a Danish pastry'.

MAKES 18

100g/3½oz/½ cup dried papaya, finely chopped

70g/2½oz/½ cup sunflower seeds, finely chopped

60g/2¼oz/½ cup finely chopped cashew nuts or almonds

160g/5½oz/2 cups wholegrain porridge oats

55g/2oz/scant ½ cup plain flour

½ tsp ground cinnamon

100g/3½oz butter

2 tbsp demerara or granulated sugar

4 tbsp clear honey or syrup (honey should not be given to children under 1 year old)

1. Preheat the oven to 150°C/300F/gas 2.
2. Mix the papaya, sunflower seeds, nuts, oats, flour and cinnamon in a bowl.
3. Melt the butter, sugar and honey in a pan. Add to the bowl and stir into a paste. Place in a 20 x 25cm/8 x 10in roasting pan lined with baking parchment. It's important that the mixture is packed together so that it sticks together once it's baked.
4. Bake in the middle of the oven for about 30 minutes, or until the the flapjack has started to colour a little at the edges. Leave to cool slightly and then cut into bars. Store in a dry place.

WALNUTS
Do try replacing the cashew nuts with walnuts. They contain omega-3, which is an essential fatty acid that the body can't produce on its own. When you cook vegetarian food it's extra important to make sure you get enough omega-3, because it can't be found in many vegetarian foods.

Choose a dairy-free margarine and use syrup instead of honey.

CANAPÉS

Four savoury and one sweet, and then you've got a complete canapé dinner, or at least an interesting selection to serve your guests when it's party time. If you need to deal with picky eaters, we suggest chunks of fruit on cocktail sticks as an alternative to the recipe below. Brush anything like apples or pears – which would otherwise go brown – with a little lemon juice.

BRIE CUBES WITH HONEY & CRUSHED NUTS

MAKES ABOUT 20

125g/4½oz/1 cup mixed nuts and seeds

1 tsp salt flakes

200g/7oz brie cheese

2 tbsp clear honey (don't give honey to children under 1 year old)

1. Toast the nuts and the seeds in a dry frying pan.
2. Blend them with a stick blender, then mix with the salt.
3. Cut the cheese into whichever shape you want your canapés to be – cubes, triangles or oblongs.
4. Warm the honey for a few seconds (in a microwave oven or a pan), so that it is runny and thin. Brush the cheese cubes with honey, then coat them with the nut mixture.
5. Store in a cool place until they're being served. These canapés are at their absolute best if they're served immediately, but they can take an hour's waiting for the guests too.

MINI BRUSCHETTAS WITH TOMATO & BASIL

MAKES ABOUT 20

5 tomatoes

1 small brown or red onion, chopped

2 garlic cloves, crushed

3½ tbsp olive oil

20–25 fresh basil leaves, chopped

salt and freshly ground black pepper

1 baguette

1. Preheat the oven to 200°C/400°C/gas 6.
2. Chop the tomatoes finely and place them in a colander to drain off some of the liquid, then place them in a bowl.
3. Add the onion, garlic, olive oil and basil leaves. Season the mixture with salt and pepper to taste and mix together.
4. Cut the baguette into slices and place on an oven rack. Toast lightly in the oven, flipping the slices over so they colour on both sides.
5. Just before serving, place a spoonful of tomato mixture on each baguette slice.

 Choose a dairy-free bread.

More recipes overleaf »

CROUSTADES WITH AVOCADO, CHILLI & LIME

MAKES ABOUT 20

2 avocados

1 small red onion, finely chopped

2 tsp finely chopped fresh chilli, or to taste
   (depending on how hot you want it)

about 1 tbsp freshly squeezed lime juice

160ml/5¼fl oz/⅔ cup crème fraîche

salt and freshly ground black pepper

about 20 croustade cases (often found on the
   shelf for crackers in the supermarket)

1. Spoon out the flesh from the avocados and dice it.
2. Mix together the avocado, onion, chilli, lime juice and crème fraîche. Season to taste with salt and pepper.
3. Spoon the filling into the croustade cases just before serving, so that the croustades don't lose their crispiness.

GREEN OLIVE PASTE WITH CAPERS

MAKES ABOUT 20

60g/2¼oz/scant ½ cup capers

150g/5½oz/1¼ cups pitted green olives

1 garlic clove

2 tbsp olive oil

salt and freshly ground black pepper

about 20 nice crackers or mini crisp bread

1. Blend the capers, olives, garlic and oil to a smooth paste, using a stick blender.
2. Season to taste with salt and pepper, but remember that capers and olives are salty anyway, so you probably won't need much salt.
3. Spoon out the paste on top of the crackers just before serving.

Choose vegan crackers.

BLUEBERRY BROWNIES

No canapé buffet is complete without a dessert canapé – everyone knows that. You can prepare these brownies in advance – they stay soft for days.

MAKES ABOUT 20 SMALL PIECES

100g/3½oz frozen or fresh blueberries

50g/1½oz butter or margarine

200g/7oz dark chocolate, broken into pieces

30g/1oz/¼ cup plain flour

1 tsp vanilla sugar

1 egg

20 walnuts, whole or chopped

mini marshmallows (optional)

1. Preheat the oven to 200°C/400°C/gas 6. Grease a 10x25cm/4x10in roasting pan.
2. Place the blueberries and butter or margarine in a pan and heat until the fat has melted. Remove from the heat, add half of the chocolate and stir until the chocolate melts.
3. Add the flour, vanilla sugar and egg and stir the mixture until smooth.
4. Pour the mixture into the prepared roasting pan and bake in the middle of the oven for 10 minutes or until the brownie has just set, but not much more than that. It's good if it's still gooey inside.
5. Melt the rest of the chocolate in a heatproof bowl set over a pan of gently simmering water, stirring until it has melted.
6. Spread the chocolate over the brownie, add the nuts and mini marshmallows, if using. Leave to set in the fridge and then cut into small squares using a sharp knife.

MINI PAVLOVAS

Portion-sized meringue nests that can be garnished according to the guests' own tastes – this might be the closest we've come to party success so far. Everyone gets to decide! Everyone is happy! Even those who are gluten intolerant, since this dessert is gluten free as long as you steer away from gluten in the toppings as well. The meringues are easy to bake, and can be made several days in advance and stored in a dry place until serving.

MAKES ABOUT 12
Meringue nests
4 egg whites
200g/7oz/1 cup caster or granulated sugar
1 tbsp cornflour
1 tsp distilled vinegar
butter, for greasing

Fruit sauce
3 passion fruits
3 tbsp lemon curd

Topping suggestions
double or whipping cream, berries or other fruit, sprinkles or sweets, nuts

MERINGUE NESTS

1. Preheat the oven to 120°C/250°F/gas ½.
2. Whisk the egg whites until stiff. Stir in the sugar and continue whisking until the mixture is shiny and can be pulled out by the whisk to form shiny peaks. Fold in the cornflour and distilled vinegar.
3. Grease circles (about 10cm/4in across) on a sheet of baking parchment. Spoon out the meringue mixture onto the circles and even them out a little.
4. Bake in the oven for 1¼ hours, then turn the oven off but leave the meringues in the oven for a few hours.

SAUCE AND TOPPING

1. Scoop out the seeds and pulp from the passion fruits into a bowl and mix with the lemon curd. The fresh, tart sauce is delicious with the sweet meringue and the cream. We usually start by adding a dollop of sauce directly onto the meringue, followed by cream, and finishing off with a small mountain of berries/nuts/sweets on top.

DO YOU WANT TO MAKE YOUR OWN LEMON CURD?

Squeeze the juice of 2 lemons and add to a pan together with 100g/3½oz/½ cup sugar and an equal quantity of butter. Warm until everything has dissolved. Whisk 2 eggs together with 100g/3½oz/½ cup sugar and add to the pan. Simmer gently while stirring constantly until everything has thickened. Important! Don't let it boil, or it will split. Store leftover lemon curd in a jar with a lid in a cool place and eat within one week.

CHOCOLATE PRALINES

Perhaps the most child-friendly baked ingredient in the world, we use oat bran instead of the standard porridge oats here, and it makes the paste a bit creamier and softer. Put simply, a little more like luxurious pralines, but still as easy to make.

1. Mix everything but the coating to a smooth paste.
2. Shape into small balls and roll in coatings of your choice. Store in a cool place.

MAKES ABOUT 30

90g/3¼oz/1 cup oat bran

120g/4¼oz/scant 1 cup plain flour

100g/3½oz/½ cup granulated or demerara sugar

20g/¾oz/scant ¼ cup cocoa powder

150g/5½oz butter, at room temperature

something nice to coat them in (see suggestions below left)

Replace the butter with dairy-free margarine and roll in a vegan coating.

COATING IDEAS:
icing sugar
vanilla sugar
sesame seeds
sprinkles
desiccated coconut
chopped nuts or almonds
melted chocolate (dip them quickly!)
cocoa powder

OAT BRAN
It's difficult to think of anything that sounds more boring than oat bran, but if you manage to look beyond the wholefood label, oat bran is actually really good stuff. For example, it can transform your completely normal chocolate ball paste into a soft praline paste. And that's just for starters! In addition, oat bran is a winner when it comes to nutrition; you could say it's a concentrated form of porridge oats: rich in vitamin E, phosphorous and iron, and last but not least, the clever little substance beta-glucan, which helps create a good environment for your blood vessels.

INDEX